CW00486828

THE BOUNDER'S
COMPANION

45°

Lock's

Belgravia Bags

Insignia

Balkan
Sobranie

Old School
(variable)

Flag

Nourishment

Snaffled

Vaulting
Ambition

Safe
Seat

Permanent
Loan

The
Chase

Foot on the Ground

THE BOUNDER

THE BOUNDER'S COMPANION

A Volume of Good Advice

HARRY CHANCE

Illustrations by ffolkes

EBURY
PRESS

This edition first published in UK in 2001 by Ebury Press

Copyright © Harry Chance 1983, 2001

1 3 5 7 9 10 8 6 4 2

Ebury Press
Random House, 20 Vauxhall Bridge Road, London SW1V 2SA

Random House Australia Pty Limited
20 Alfred Street, Milsons Point, Sydney, New South Wales 2061, Australia

Random House New Zealand Limited
18 Poland Road, Glenfield, Auckland 10, New Zealand

Random House South Africa (Pty) Limited
Endulini, 5A Jubilee Road, Parktown 2193, South Africa

Random House UK Limited Reg. No. 954009

A CIP catalogue record for this book is available from the British Library

ISBN 0 09 188300 8

Jacket design by Jon Gray
Image courtesy of The Kobal Collection

Typeset by SX Typesetting
Printed and bound in Great Britain by Mackays of Chatham plc, Chatham, Kent

Papers used by Ebury Press are natural, recyclable products made from wood
grown in sustainable forests.

To my wives
and Susan Hill,
without whom none of this
would have been passable

Contents

Preface

The human landscape in the 21st century presents a bleak and tedious prospect. Vast grey masses of people, some overweight and many starving, jostle on the land masses and dot the oceans in task forces, oil rigs and refugee hulks. Here and there among the seething rabble, however, there are eminences – men clear of eye and grey of temple, dressed in regimental ties, tweed suits and black brogues from Ganes, smoking fat cigars with the bands on. Round their brogues suitors mill. The eminences pay no attention. The wrinkled sea beneath them crawls. They are looking out for number one; they are the bounders.

A bounder is a person who has by unremitting self-discipline and attention to detail achieved a spiritual state comparable with that of a bedbug. The rewards are obvious: wealth, power and fame are his, and all without a stroke of work. *Si monumentum requiris, circumspice*, or, if you prefer, look at me.

The bounder is fulfilling the ultimate desire of many of the human race, which is to lie in the sun while other people work and worry. I hope that in the pages that follow you will find some pointers to making your own life more fulfilling. At least that is what the publishers told me to say. Now that you have paid your money, I can reveal that I do not give a goddamn about your spiritual welfare, or any other aspect of your progress, come to that. The proceeds of this book are now safe in the Caymans; say no more.

Job descriptions of bounders are many and glamorous. Some are doctors, lawyers or clergymen; others are journalists; some again – an enormous number – are politicians. Their heads bob jauntily as they interview suitors; their faces are creased with smiles and their brains are thick with plots.

Bounders think, *all the time*. On their feet, on their backs and in their chairs.

They also talk. Bounders have invented a thing called the New Respectability, which has put them quite simply in a class of their own. It used to be that any member of a class could become a bounder by attempting to emulate the habits of any other class;

thus coal heavers put up the backs of dukes by attempting to dine with them, and marquesses put mill girls in impossible positions with proposals of marriage. Now, however, bounders constitute the only pure class there is; the non-bounding classes merge into a huge grey lump, and seethe at the feet of the eminences (see above).

This has naturally inspired many non-bounders to take themselves in hand. Poor fools, many of them. Not a chance. Atavistic emotions, outmoded conventions like love and pity corrupt and sway even some of the most promising from the path. Many are called, but few are chosen. The majority will simply go under, too stupid, too decent to survive. Others, more dedicated but lacking the call, will become members of one of the subspecies which are to true bounders as Hottentot warriors are to the Knights of the Round Table.

Perhaps it is worth discussing these subspecies at this point, since by pointing out their shortcomings, we may arrive at a definition of the pure bounder. They are: cads, wastrels, arrivistes, parvenus and bullies. Often these types are thought of as synonymous with bounders. But, as any bounder worth his salt will tell

11

you, once you have bought him enough drinks, they are nothing of the kind. Theirs is a narrow, uninspired approach.

Cads tend to be violent, particularly towards women. Purist bounders shun violence, except to children, as they are blessed with the healthy, life-preserving instinct of *sheer cowardice*.

Wastrels have plenty of money and talent, which they abuse. Bounders have neither, but abuse the substitutes they have invented. They take *posititve pride in not having it*, but in spending it all the same.

Arrivistes are obsessed by the idea of getting somewhere. Since a bounder who is bounding correctly must be entirely self-satisfied at all times, he knows that wherever he is is, by definition, the best place for him to be. Arrivistes get ulcers; bounders, except when they have their reasons for faking them (see page 82), do not.

Parvenus have arrived already. Many parvenus have been bounders in their day; but the perfect tense in the participle implies that their bounding days are over and that they are now resigned to a life of soggy, complacent inertia. While complacency is a fine asset for a bounder, and inertia an enviable if temporary state, they are not in themselves enough.

Bullies are handicapped by their predilection for physical violence and, given the feelings of inferiority which lie at the root of their vocation, lack complacency. A good bully can with time and work become a reasonable all-round bounder but will never make the first team, or the Cabinet as it is sometimes called.

Nobody is more vividly aware than I that about half the world is composed of the female sex. Over the years it has become apparent that this sex is able to bound just as efficiently as the male. Here, too, there are lesser categories.

Bitches have taught society to monger rumours and season its fricasses with ground glass. Their hallmark is an admirable cunning combined with an almost fiendish sang-froid. It is to be deplored that all their clever remarks are made not for their personal advantage but simply to make other people miserable. Of course, this can be very satisfying, but it smacks of unselfishness and is hardly, one suspects, worth the trouble.

Adventuresses may occasionally become accomplished bounders. The classic fault of the adventuress is that she doesn't know when to stop and let dignified sloth take the place of the upward hustle.

To those who fall into neither of these categories and are thirsty for wisdom, let me say this: if in *The Bounder's Companion* I address my remarks nominally to the male sex, this is only for convenience; the advice it contains applies to ladies – women, as many of you now call yourselves – as much as to men. If your wits are too gummed up with hormones to make the sexual transposition, tough.

Long and gruelling study has led me to the conviction that a human being is the sum of his character defects. Victorian moralists and similar pie-in-the-sky purveyors stress that humans should rise above their faults. Happily, we have progressed beyond these fallacies. As Werner Erhart, inventor of Est and perhaps the greatest bounding coach of all time, once said: 'You are all beautiful, but especially me.'

In this book, I have laid out a path for all to follow. If you cannot master it, then I can only say, in the nicest possible way, that you are even more stupid then I thought. When you start to flag, remember this: reputable physicians claim that after Armageddon the world will be populated exclusively by rats, cockroaches and various grasses. They are wrong. The grasses, filled with gambolling rats and roaches, will also rustle over the shiny black brogues and impeccable heather mixture turnups of the bounders.

Bound, then, and survive.

1
Bound for Glory

I am frequently asked how it is that I am such an unmitigated bounder. It is my habit to reply, modestly, that in my case it is a matter of innate talent combined with constant application. Since there appears to be some confusion in the public mind as to what exactly a bounder is, I think I cannot do better than to outline my career to date – not as an exercise in self-adulation, though it will undoubtedly look like that, but as what old Henry Buffett who taught me Greek might have called a paradigm.

I was born in the Home Counties at about the time Neville Chamberlain was standing on the aeroplane steps after his flight from Munich, waving his little piece of paper. My mother used to say in later life that there was a good deal of Chamberlain in me. At the time I was not sure what she meant, but later I began to suspect there might have been a little bit of Chamberlain in her. Nine months before my arrival she was the undisputed toast of the Purley golf club dance. My mother was a creature with the strong passions one would expect of a fourteenth cousin nine times removed of the Duke of Marlborough. My father would have been pursuing his researches in the bar, recovering as always from a hard day's regulating the human resources of England's capital.* Chequers was a short distance down the road; the moon was full. Mindful of my mother's reputation, I shall say no more.

I must confess that my titular father is a shadowy, ill-remembered figure. At first his work kept him from home at all hours. Later, a change of career landed him in the clandestine intelligence serves, so that we were forced to deny all knowledge of his whereabouts when questioned by enemy agents disguised as tradesmen, bookies and the like. As far as I can remember he was an extremely happy man, with no trace of that moping spirit that lets the problems of others detract from its *joie de vivre*. I have followed his example faithfully.

I owe him two debts of gratitude: first, for teaching me that it is a waste of time to stand around explaining

---

* A presumed reference to Mr Albert Chance, a bus conductor of Purley, dismissed for intemperance, July 1939.

something if it is possible to walk away; secondly, for the speculation on the fringes of the Groundnut Scheme that made it possible for me to attend both Eton College and Christ Church, Oxford. These debts I would willingly repay were it not for my policy of never repaying debts if I can avoid so doing. He must be pretty old and slow by now.

By the time I went to school, I was quietly confident of my ability to make my way in the world. Perhaps I was lucky in having one of those characters that formed early. This made for stability in the growing boy, and a calm, reflective puberty. During my time at Eton, a savage and deeply frightening place, I developed self-assurance and charm to a marked degree. I also realized the basic stupidity of courage, a revelation which enabled me in later life to stay protectively with the ladies while members of my own sex were dealing with shipwreck, civil insurrection and so forth. Finally, my imagination, always lively, stood me in good stead when I was forced to avoid the unpleasant consequences of several almost completely innocent actions.

It was at school, too, that I learned about work. All around me boys were struggling to digest huge volumes of fact and opinion. It seemed to me ludicrously wasteful that so many minds should be learning, as it were, in step. I therefore devoted myself to social life, allowing boys really interested in acquiring knowledge and smaller than myself to graft on my behalf. As a result, I earned the triumphant accolade of a public school education. In the eyes of authority, complete facelessness; in the eyes of my fellow pupils, awe and respect.

Though reasonably comfortable, Eton presented a few problems. It is a considerable feat of management for the untrained mind to maintain a string of academic assistants through threats and bribery alone. The central skills of untruthfulness and trickery are stretched to creaking. After this, Oxford was a pleasant three-year holiday. Facilities for poker, racing and general relaxation were unrivalled. In addition, credit was freely available at Blackwell's bookshop and in the tailors' establishments of the High. The rich and gullible abounded. Here I widened my acquaintance with the right sort of people and started the collection of ties and blazers which has been worth more than an oil well to me. In panelled rooms above Peck Quad, drunken

Grid fellows shovelled money into my pockets. At Schools, I secured a brilliant aegrotat with the co-operation of a medical student who was under the impression my father owned the Mayo Clinic. The world lay at my feet.

I walked all over it.

My subsequent career has been neatly described as rich and varied. During its course I have, naturally, been in the City. I have also, naturally, been in politics. I have been a guest of Her Majesty and sold used Vauxhalls in Catford, experiences among the richest available to any human being. I have travelled the world in the company of numerous beautiful women, including my lucky, lovely wives. Nowadays, I divide my time between Bali, Aruba, the Cayman Islands, Miami Beach and Wentworth. My working days are over, and in my sunset years – for I am now forty-five – I feel, like many great artists, the need to confide my method to history. Milton probably felt the same way, also Shakespeare.

But Milton was blind and Shakespeare was bald. I have 20-20 vision and a full head of hair. You may draw your own conclusions as to who is right.

2
Bounder's Briefing

A little while ago I met in Jules Bar in Jermyn Street an acquaintance with an excellent job in one of London's most profitable advertising agencies. Noticing that he was drinking a very acceptable Krug, I joined him. When I had finished the bottle and was helping him order another, I asked him what he was celebrating. He told me that having gone as far as the agency could take him, he was about to marry the chairman's daughter and devote himself to what he described as 'the life of Riley'.

Naturally I was concerned for the fellow. He was improperly dressed, in the sunglasses, closely cropped black beard and American lorry-driver's cap peculiar to his profession. Beneath the euphoria induced by good fortune and Krug, I sensed a tentativeness.

It is true that professions, or more correctly, jobs, such as advertising and politics provide a useful introduction to my vocation (see Chapter 3); but to suggest that an account executive or creative group supremo can, by the simple expedient of giving up work, become an accomplished bounder is like suggesting that the sculptor Praxiteles chipped out the Phryne *Cupid* after a few days' whittling balsa wood at his preparatory school. The aptitude will be there, but the craftsmanship will not be developed.

I cannot stress too strongly that self-education should begin with the onset of consciousness and should not ease until consciousness itself ceases. Bounding is a spiritual discipline similar to and in some cases identical with that taught by Swami Baghwan and Guru Maharaj Ji. You will know at an early age if you have the vital seed of innate talent. Develop it!

With a view to this, I sketched a few ideas for my friend. He was extraordinarily grateful and asked me to be best man at the wedding. I declined, contenting myself instead with his fiancée's telephone number. She turned out to be a charming girl, talented sexually and easily as rich as my friend had described her. The educational hints that follow, a fuller version of my earlier advice to him, were composed by me in her father's attractive villa overlooking Tangier in the few free moments I had during my negotiations to sell her to an oil magnate. Eventually I decided not to send them to my friend but sold them to my publishers for many thousands of pounds. I am now convinced that I did the right thing. Bounders generally are.

THE BOUNDING BABY

It has often struck me, on the rare occasions I have been forced into the company of young children, that each of us is born a bounder. A chap I know who had a fortune-telling business near Epsom used to claim that young babies know everything, and 'learning' is a process of forgetting rather than acquiring new knowledge. One can see his point. The behaviour of a new-born child, grabbing at breasts, making motions suggestive of drinking, staying awake all night and sleeping much of the day, is strongly reminiscent of many of my friends. Teach a new-born baby to play roulette and you would probably have the most accomplished bounder the world has ever seen.

There are, however, problems. Among these are lack of mobility and the inability of tiny kidneys to cope with a decent quantity of whisky. Also the immaturity of the intellect may lead to poor manners and deficient bowel control. The duty of the parent must therefore be to develop the child's intellect by what is called *stimulation*. It is well known that babies learn just about everything they know from their mothers. A useful regime stresses self-interest: the child's first question should be 'What's in it for *me*?'

Thus an educational programme is easily mapped out. Babies should not be bought toys, as the process of stealing from their fellow mites develops self-reliance and a respect for property. Correct emotional development can be ensured by constant quarrelling in the baby's presence. It is necessary to teach babies to keep quiet; in later life important deals may be prejudiced by blabbing. While some may aver that isolation is the best silencer, my experience points to fear being the key. Clumps on the ear or electric shocks may at first produce yelling, but in the long term they will have their reward and they do possess the added advantage of instilling a decent timidity at an early stage. And without timidity, as Mrs Iscariot could probably assure us were she alive today, there can be no real deviousness.

By the time a firm foundation of fear, distrust and avarice is well established, your child should be walking. Now comes the first onset of social activity. Once upon a time this was orchestrated by nannies, and took place almost exclusively in the dignified surrounds of Kensington Gardens. Since the recent unfortunate slide in social standards, the toddler is likely to find himself enmeshed in playgroups, crèches and the like in which he is expected to interact meaningfully with his peers (who are depressingly unlikely to be peers in any true sense of the word). This presents the first opportunity to display anything like style or panache, and represents the end of the parents' responsibility towards the child. From now on, you are on your own.

The general aim, at this point, should be to make the best possible impact on the Montessori teacher or other child minder while getting as much of one's own way as possible. Since it is pretty unlikely that any bounder will be able to read before the age of about fourteen, persuade your parents at this stage to read you *Little Lord Fauntleroy*. Note the conduct of Little Lord F. towards the Earl and his dog. This is very much the sort of thing that is expected of you by the adult world. Meanwhile, if caring parents can provide a junior biography of Mr Bernard Cornfeld or Robert Vesco, little folk will acquire some valuable pointers to useful behaviour towards their fellow children.

Everyday social intercourse can be guided by simple self-interest. Children's parties, however, are high spots and should be approached with real enthusiasm, providing as they do rare learning opportunities. Games in particular provide important hints as to the conduct of your future life. They fall into two principal categories.

1 *Games of violence* These include hunt-the-thimble, musical chairs and blind-man's-buff. They involve much rushing about, and small prizes scarcely worth the risk of physical injury (is any prize?). Avoiding them may lead to accusations of shirking. The best bet is usually to claim to have twisted your leg in a dangerous but non-specific manner *immediately after the food*, which usually precedes games. This will provide a fine opportunity to polish off the remnants of the meal and also, since these things are usually birthday parties, to browse through the presents,

selecting those which catch the fancy. It is an established fact that gift cataloguing at children's parties is lax.

2 *Games of cunning*   These include pass-the-parcel, lotto, pin-the-tail-on-the-donkey, etc., and are valuable training for important features of later life such as billiards. Affect a cheerful insouciance and declare that the game's the thing and you for one are terribly bad at it. Make sure that you have with you a duplicate parcel, set of lotto cards or map of the donkey. When you win, affect surprise. If you are caught, cause confusion. If you are unable to do so in a room full of three-year-olds on pleasure bent, you are unworthy of the name of trainee bounder and should transfer ambitions to the West Yorkshire Constabulary or some town planning department.

A word of caution here: you are at your most vulnerable between the ages of zero and four. The pathetic liberals who now control every aspect of life have given new credence to the ancient fallacy that small children are charming, worth talking to, etc. People will talk to you with a freedom you will seldom again encounter whilst sober. Exploit this and remember: when in doubt, ask yourself 'What's in it for *me?*'

THE SLIMY SCHOOLBOY

A young acquaintance of mine told me a story the other day which I think sums up all that is best about one's schooldays. It seems that he returned from the holidays with his right arm tattooed from wrist to armpit. Hitherto he had been known as The Toad and not, as far as I could gather, greatly popular. The tattoos changed everything. His schoolmates were full of admiration. A craze started. Within the week, forty-three boys had slipped away to nearby parlours and submitted to the needle. At this point my acquaintance took soap and water and washed off his own tattoos which, it transpired, had been applied in poster colours by his father's kittenish mistress in Monte Carlo. Bound by the school's absurd honour code, not one of the forty-three revealed the instigator of the craze. They were shipped en masse to a skin hospital for lengthy grafts and laser treatment. In the absence of

competition, my acquaintance thus found himself promoted to head boy. What is more, he was the youngest head boy the school had ever had, and the fact was inscribed in letters of gold against his name on the assembly hall plaques. This will, I am convinced, only serve to his advantage.

Of course, not all our fathers' mistresses can paint. But it is the principle of the thing that counts – any boy cunning enough to stay on top in the difficult and dangerous society of a British preparatory school should not rest on his laurels. He should manoeuvre to excel.

The Bounder's Companion

STAFF

The senior staff of preparatory schools provides excellent behavioural examples, though unfortunately these are largely negative. Many fine arms salesmen and Members of Parliament have felt the urge to give it all up and start a preparatory school. Most resist the urge, realizing that it calls for contact with the more depressing type of human being, and also that it gives hundreds of eager young minds an opportunity to study their technique at close quarters.

Junior masters are different. Many of my circle have spent periods of rest and refreshment teaching imperfect French and history at establishments in the Southwest. There is a soothing anonymity, and often enough a busty young matron. The smell of chalk dust and dubbin acts as a tonic to a brain wearied by the rattle of Jermyn Street and Royal Ascot. To be perfectly honest (which I never am), I have done a bit of it myself, once spending a whole school year teaching Hindi to a first-year French class without anyone noticing the difference.

Bounder's Briefing

THE AIMS OF THE PREPARATORY SCHOOL

Most schools claim to do things like Stress the Development of the Whole Boy, with particular reference to Steeplechasing and Physics. Few believe this, least of all intelligent pupils and masters. The true aim is, of course, to make money for the proprietors by ramming pupils into prestigious public schools (see Appendix One). It is obviously desirable to go to a decent public school, if only on a visit to sing at a choir festival in the chapel and acquire some useful slang in the process. So the sensible pupil will avoid games, take reasonable precautions when preparing for common entrance (hand-held access to the internet can be of inestimable use during exams), and look as if he is following the course laid out for him by his elders. All the time he will be keeping his eyes open, and showing that although his fellows may be cleverer, more athletic and generally more interested than he, he has tremendous depth and is likely to go far.

One useful indicator is to have your uniform made by a good tailor or, better still, couturier. Yves Saint Laurent can do remarkable things with grey flannel shorts. Gucci football boots give a *je ne sais quoi* of distinction to the Colts Second XI. A Chippendale tuck box is a *sine qua non*. And no dormy feast is worth a damn unless the pyjamas of the revellers are silk, by Charvet.

THE INGRATIATING ADOLESCENT

Statistics show that it is around puberty that one makes the friends most likely to endure for the remainder of one's life. This is recognized in African

societies through such organizations as circumcision clubs. Fortunately these have lost popularity in more civilized communities, though it is fair to say that entry into some public schools carries almost as much risk to the genitalia.

Public schools differ from preparatory schools in that they resemble the real world more closely. Many of the better ones are to a large extent governed by the pupils, the masters exercising supervision from a distance. I always like to draw an analogy here with later life – the pupils representing clubs, professional associations and so on, and the masters representing the police force and the government. I have already made reference to my conviction that the correct way to conduct oneself is to take advantage of one's fellow pupils without, if possible, making any mark on the memory of the staff.

The inmates of public schools are, superficially, a highly critical lot. They tend to observe keenly and comment freely on matters such as accent, dress and behaviour. Surveys show, however, that the self-consciousness of adolescence can be exploited to great effect by anyone wishing to short-circuit this scrutiny.

I well remember escaping the consequences of an ill-considered south London vowel sound by donning rapidly a new tie in coral-pink silk with a motif of lime-green horseshoes which aroused such admiration among my fellow Etonians that the whole matter was forgotten forthwith.

Public schools are basically a matter of hormones. I am assuming that very few of us are hormonally average, and that puberty comes either embarrassingly early or embarrassingly late. This seems to be the case with almost all bounders. If the former, one's popularity is assured. Go into a nearby town and find a pregnant woman of the poorer class. Promise her money if she will walk with you through the school precincts. Afterwards, pay her or not, as you will (I know what I would), and spread the rumour (see Chapter 7) that she is the matron of your preparatory school and that you are responsible for her condition. In these difficult times a promise of money can do a lot to cheer a member of the working class, especially a pregnant one.

If late puberty is a problem, there is only one solution: join the choir. All public schools administer a voice test immediately new boys arrive. Do your level best to pass it, disregarding old sweats who tell you about the boredom of choir practice, the importunities of the upper school and so on. In the view of many accomplished bounders there is no finer training than to pipe Handel while dressed in ruff and surplice and thinking monstrous thoughts. It is one of the best and earliest exercises in not letting your right hand know what your left hand doeth. Encourage the upper school; you will be able to use it against them one day. By the time your voice breaks you will be streets ahead of the rabble outside the choir stalls. Also, you will have experience of belonging to a small, predatory group within a group, which is, after all, what we are talking about.

After a couple of years at school you will be expected to have settled in and become merry, darting and plucky. These are qualities entirely out of tune with the times, having originated in the days when the sun never set over the British Empire; even then, they excited the mirth of Chinese and Nigerian tribal chiefs. But as these foreign folk soon discovered, they serve as excellent masks for the more primitive attributes of mendacity, trickiness and blame-shifting. I therefore propose to discuss them individually.

MERRINESS

The seed of the bonhomie you will be expected to display in later life. Centrally, merriness is a matter of making people laugh. Of course, this is not always easy, particularly for those of us who are naturally dignified. There are, however, many excellent books of jokes available and half an hour a night under the bedclothes with a torch will rapidly build up a fine repertoire. Connections with the City of London are also useful in this respect, as the duplicating machines of EC1 are famous for producing a line of cheerful humour which would give the Obscene Publications Squad coronaries. Jokes at the expense of others are particularly recommended, the more so if your butt is old and/or crippled. A friend of mine attributes his current status as chairman of a breakfast television company to the confidence boost induced by setting fire to his scoutmaster, a dotard who had sustained a serious knee injury at Rorke's Drift.

DARTINGNESS

Perhaps the least definable of schoolboy qualities. It develops the quickness on your feet so important for the awkward situations in which you might find yourself in later life; but it is not necessarily a physical quality. If, for instance, youthful exuberance has just impelled you to hurl half a brick through the fourteen-century stained glass of the chapel's east window, the correctly darting schoolboy will not run, nor will he drop flat on his face in the long grass and wait for retribution like any amphibian beneath the harrow. He will realize that there are two choices: to blame a meteorite and cover himself in glory in the eyes of the physics master (more than likely an anticlerical in his own right); or to blame the stupidest person he can see – there will be no shortage at any well-run public school. Whichever the case, he should stick to his story, even under cross-examination. Was it not Voltaire who said, 'Never apologize, never explain'? Perhaps one could define dartingness as the capacity to leap for safe ground and, having once reached it, to stick to it like a limpet.

PLUCK
One of those so-called viruses thinking people recognize as redundant, being often in direct conflict with self-preservation. The appearance of pluck can, however, be extremely beneficial to one's social standing, a fact well known to those intrepid Members of Parliament, strangers to self-interest, who are regularly besieged by journalists during attempts to make safe the fabric of civilization by denouncing nail varnish as a fire risk after air crash horror kills 180. With a little imagination, stubbornness can be made to look like pluck. The only thing I can give you is to ask yourself, confronted with a difficult and dangerous situation, what a backbench MP of any party (but preferably Conservative) would do. If you consistently come up with the right answer, you are well on your way.

UNIFORMS
Unthinking rebels at good public schools often create a quite unnecessary fuss about uniforms. While some, such as those worn at Christ's Hospital, are actively

embarrassing, most are quite inoffensive. (The only solution at Christ's Hospital is to arrange to have yourself expelled without delay – see below.) There is no finer common ground in later life than a group discussion about a uniform. If you discover a prince of the blood who also remembers Steggles who used to keep ferrets in his boater at Harrow, you are as good as in his polo team.

WRONG ATTITUDE

There is an awful lot of wrong attitude at most public schools. It finds expression in slovenly dress, independent thinking and questioning of values. Wrong attitude has no place in the life of a trainee bounder. Your task is not to question the values of your school but to use them as a series of interlinked trampolines up which you will bound to apotheosis.

EXPULSION

Expulsion is merely falling off the trampoline (see above) and is seldom fatal. It can, however, be disagreeable, particularly when accompanied by physical violence. Much tension can be released by screaming and blubbering under the lash. Afterwards, as the storm clears and the wounds heal, new vistas will become apparent. Take a positive attitude: most people only go to one public school. A really skilled expellee, however, can go to as many as six, and acquire membership of old boys' associations of all. It is true that the nature of schools that will accept the expellee changes after the first couple, but there are compensations. A godson of mine found himself after a record eight expulsions at a maximum security public school in the Orkneys. His visions of inhospitable climate and rigorous discipline were swiftly dispelled when he arrived and found himself among the sons of the entire Iraqi military elite and the offspring of three senior members of the St Petersburg mafia. He has never looked back. With contacts like those, one would hardly expect him to.

VALE, ALMA MATER!
The final year at public school is an exciting time. Drink becomes available in quantity, and maturity and poise

bring a new meaning to encounters with members of the opposite sex. These are important in your education, but immoderate indulgence may irritate those in authority over you. Having spent four years escaping the notice of members of staff, now is the time to be ingratiating. But keep a sense of proportion – it is foolishness to imagine that buying the headmaster lunch at the Connaught in term time will make him remember you as anyone other than the person who should be punished for evading the nourishing gammon, cabbage and mash provided in the boys' canteen. Basic errors of this kind indicate that your judgement is not of the standard required for real success in the wider world.

It is also unwise to stray too far in the opposite direction. One of my own contemporaries, returning from a diverting evening in a nearby gaming hell, had the ill luck to meet his housemaster by the dustbins at the foot of the fire escape leading back into the house. Thinking swiftly, he coshed the man with a heavy torch, but was horrified to find that the master had failed to become unconscious. The poor fellow was expelled. I met him afterwards in Hanover Square, where he was working as a traffic warden, and he averred that it had been unpardonable not to have been carrying an iron bar or a sock full of sand. I realized at that point that the fellow was doomed, lacking as he did the basic reserves of cowardice to seek refuge in penitent weeping.

LEAVING PRESENTS

The more studious type of master enjoys receiving books, pleasantly bound and of suitable antiquity. If, however, you have managed to avoid learning to read, it is probably safer to present him with a small but costly item from somewhere like Asprey's. The association in the headmaster's mind of your name with a lump of precious metal in his possession cannot fail to be of importance when, in later life, he is asked for references by prospective parents-in-law or probation officers.

THE KEY OF THE DOOR

In my day, one had to wait for one's twenty-first birthday before one was regarded as an adult. With the lowering of the age to eighteen, new horizons open. While some regard it as sad that it is now impossible to hold one's parents responsible for one's debts during one's time at university, others breathe a sigh of relief. For, of course, it is by no means essential to go to university nowadays, even if one has secured the requisite qualifications. The arguments break down as follows:

– there are only two universities in England: Oxford and Cambridge. I believe there are other establishments, known as 'red brick' and 'fibreglass', extensively patronized by the middle classes, but it is unwise to be associated with these as nobody of any significance will be met there.

– it is rather difficult to get into Oxford and Cambridge.

– if you go to a university, you are missing out three years which could otherwise be spent getting ahead. Very few of the top-flight arms salesmen or racing drivers one meets have degrees. The only exception to this rule is politics, for which the Oxford Union, home of some truly remarkable bounders, seems to be a *sine qua non.*

A SERVANT OF HER MAJESTY

If one is given to nostalgia one can easily waste large segments of one's life wishing one was alive in 1850, and in possession of HM commission. It must have been a wonderful existence: plenty of drink, plenty of cards and little to do except whisk rich and willing fillies from under the noses of their mammas. In those happy days one man in hussar's uniform was as good as, or at least scarcely distinguishable from, another. It was taken for granted that you would be drunk and in debt. There was, of course, no question of fighting.

Nowadays, all that has changed. The army is a dreary and middle-class affair, admitting as much when it calls its men 'the professionals'. My friend George Stimson very nearly did himself an injury passing their interviews, only to find himself shut up in an iron box on Salisbury Plain. He was forced to stand for Parliament in order to get himself out of the mess, and is now hotly tipped for Cabinet rank. Full of initiative,

George, but weak on judgement. He should go far.

The last flurry of the great days of military power was National Service. I admit that after I had done time at Eton and Oxford I was seriously out of touch with the Great Unwashed. But a mere six months after securing my commission I was in a bunker in the Rhineland discussing with a former shop steward from Burnley the ethics of selling a late model Centurion to the East Germans. He was of the opinion that the Red Bloc was unlikely to have the cash and would have philosophical objections to hire purchase. At my suggestion they finally paid in vodka, but that is another story. What I am trying to say is that National Service did wonders for the initiative, and we shall not see its like again.

A GUEST OF HER MAJESTY

It never fails to amaze me that HM Prisons are run by the Home Office rather than the Department of Education. In the absence of National Service, they fulfil the same place in the development of the young male of a certain class as Swiss finishing schools fulfilled in the development of two of my wives.

A word of warning: there exists a type of person who is unable to see the research value of porridge and will take it as an adverse comment passed by society on your *modus vivendi*. Prudence therefore suggests that your curriculum vitae should make no reference to your spell inside. If anyone seeing you after your release comments on your absence from the scene and asks why you are looking pale, fit and have shorter hair than usual, explain that you have been seeking the mother lode north of Disko Bay, Greenland. You may even be able to sell him shares in the mine.

Typical timing of a spell at one of our excellent penal institutions is as follows: after the termination of the previous stage of one's formal education, one should devote oneself to the amassing of capital. Suitable schemes are mail order, property speculation or the promotion of mining companies. On exposure, await the police with crossed arms and a light smile. Why worry? You will previously have salted away your couple of million in a Swiss bank and there is no danger of your getting more than twelve months unless, of course, you have injured somebody physically, in which case you are insufficiently timid and deserve what is coming to you. Counsel for the prosecution may harp disagreeably about the widows, orphans, etc., now selling matches in the Haymarket as a result of your machinations. Pay no attention. His speech, like that of the judge, is a mere formality. The widows and orphans should be thought of as taxpayers, advancing your education by means of a grant. Meanwhile, maintain your innocence and relieve your feelings by blubbering while being sentenced.

Once within the gates of a penal institution, show willing. It may be that you will have sympathetic friends who were at school with the governor, and that they will have written him many letters. This, allied to the fact that prison officers are only human and that you are considerably richer than they, should make it fairly easy for you to ease into a position of trust and influence.

The traditional berth of men of intelligence and initiative is the prison library. A sample of strategy for arriving here is as follows: you are permitted one snapshot of an approved loved one. Resist the urge to stick up pictures of female acquaintances without their clothes. They give a déclassé atmosphere to any cell and are unlikely to encourage anyone except common criminals. Instead, ask a friend to send a double-sided frame bearing on one face a portrait of Ann Widdecombe, and on the other a signed photograph of a liberal Anglican such as the Bishop of Chester. When being visited by the authorities, make sure that Widdecombe is showing and turn the discussion to law enforcement. Stress the desirability of bringing back the lash, rope and rack. Always refer to her as 'St Ann' and reminisce at length about your discussions with her concerning the problems of inner-city policing. At your trial your defence counsel will already have publicized the fact that you are an intelligent person of enormous promise fallen into hands of feckless and unscrupulous manipulators. Express as much contrition as is consistent with the fact that none of it was your fault. However tempted, do not under any circumstances offer share options in enterprises you plan after your release. After a few months, prison officials will be using you as something between a confessional and an oracle. They are, however, a suspicious breed, and you may have to apply side-strain. This is where the Bishop of Chester comes in.

Since the abolition of the death penalty, chaplains have gone downhill. They tend to be embarrassingly eager and pitiably socialist; a right-thinking multiple murderer taking up his position on the trap would scorn the prayers of such milksops. But prison officers nowadays pander increasingly to sociologists, and often the chaplain is the only sociologist on the block. So engage him in discussions on the merits of the Series 3 prayer book and the rewriting of the hymn book. At an appropriate point, remark casually that you see your period of rehabilitation as a ideal opportunity to carry out a scheme which has long been near your heart, namely to rewrite the Old Testament without reference to outmoded concepts such as kings, principalities, powers or a fuddy-duddy, authoritarian, paternalistic-type deity. Before you can say 'Lo, the Angel of the Lord', you will be ensconced at a comfortable table near the library radiator, while your cellmates sew mail bags, strive in the gardens, or paint hideous and confusing motorway signs. If the authorities ask you what you are up to, admit that you are rewriting the Old Testament, but claim you are doing this to remove disagreeable passages concerning peace and love. Any work you are forced to accomplish on this project will take precious little of your time, so, in order to beguile the passing hours, try a mind-strengthening project: write pornographic reminiscences of snoozes with the aristocracy and sell them to your fellow prisoners for tobacco.

So much for dignified survival. But there is more to prison life: there exists in penal institutions a vast storehouse of knowledge that is simply not available anywhere else. The overcrowding that currently exists may at first seem unpleasant to one used to privacy and silk pyjamas, but it does result in a constant exchange of useful information. Conversation with your fellows will fill any gaps in your knowledge left by a first-class education. A journeyman bounder can rub along in the City with a simple knowledge of basic financial practice, some attractive share certificates and a couple of rich and influential friends. But the bounder with a knowledge of safe-cracking, computer fraud and elementary mugging can hardly help rising to the top of his profession.

This was borne out by a chap who lives just down the road from my house in Wentworth. When he emerged into the world from a two-year stretch for fraud he found that an extremely rich great-aunt had that day handed in her dinner pail. This unsympathetic female had always hated him, and once had cheerfully shown him her will to reinforce the point that he had nothing to expect. How foolish of her. My friend had noticed that the contents of the safe were bequeathed intact to a cousin of his who had been unfortunate enough to contract muscular dystrophy. The will-reading was scheduled for the Tuesday after my friend's release date. He proceeded to the great aunt's home, effected an easy entry and opened the combination lock of the safe using methods he had learned in the metalwork shop at Parkhurst, IOW. Pocketing the cash and jewels he found, he inserted a note in the great-aunt's handwriting, advising the cousin to adopt a health-food diet and hope for the best. (Since his mind-strengthening calligraphy classes at Parkhurst, he found it easy to write in almost any handwriting, including that of the chief cashier of the Bank of England.) My friend then visited certain small jewellers' shops not far from Brick Lane, about which one of his cellmates had told him, where he was able to dispose of the jewellery. With the proceeds he set up as an estate agent in southeast London, where a small but lucrative part of his business is the letting for periods ranging from nine months to thirty years, of the large houses inhabited by various thickset businessmen whose acquaintance he made in prison. Now as wealthy and idle as anyone could wish, he freely admits that had he not done his porridge he would probably still be a curate in Basingstoke embezzling the little envelopes from the collection plate.

With your release from the prison of your choice, your formal education is at an end. By now you should be more than a match for anyone you chance to meet, and keen to prove it. From now on you will walk softly, across the bodies of adversaries and friends alike.

INFORMAL EDUCATION

It has not escaped my attention that there are one or two people walking the West End of London who have, for one reason or another, failed to progress through the private educational system. They fall, as I see it, into three main categories.

1 *The poor*   Since an education is expensive and all
too frequently left in the hands of incompetent
agencies such as parents, some people find themselves
without one, or 'given' one by the State, which amounts
to the same thing. Few of these will make good
bounders since even the most talented will, by
definition, be parvenus or arrivistes.

2 *The stupid*   While many bounders consider it
unnecessary to be able to read or write more than their
own alias on a cheque, the general trend is these days
towards literacy. Many have achieved tolerable success
even though they have left school at the age of sixteen
or, in extreme cases, have never been to school at all.
This last category can often achieve surprising
excellence, since their wits have been honed to razor
keenness by truancy. They do, however, need an
exceptional cover story. Two that spring to mind are:
having been tutored secretly from infancy by Richard
Dawkins or having been raised by a herd of gazelles in
the western Sahara.

3 *The latecomers*   At the beginning of the chapter I

The Bounder's Companion

discussed the case of my friend who, having gone to the limit in the advertising profession, was taking up bounding as a second career. Despite his lack of success, it is my firm opinion that he had the right notion. Given the tendency of the so-called 'glamour professions' to spit out their whizzkids well chewed at the age of thirty or so, and given the psychological characteristics necessary for entry into a 'glamour profession', ex-whizzkids sometimes make excellent bounders. All that is required is a little retrospective opportunity enhancement.

I have devised a scheme of informal education which, I hope, will solve some of the problems experienced by members of these three categories in building themselves a secure past. It will also be of use to those who have had the benefit of a full education of the better type, but who have since fallen victim to alcoholic amnesia.

(i) *Nomenclature* Very few people bother to check Debrett's or parish registers nowadays when assessing new companions. This is an enormous advantage to those who wish to arrive in society fully formed, like Venus on the half-shell but better dressed. Also, since recent statistical discoveries show that some 60 per cent of the population can trace their descent from Edward II, claims to aristocratic connections are not only easy to make but have a six-to-four chance of being legitimate. If, however, you are unlucky enough to come from a long line of Harijan lascars, the *Almanach de Gotha* will provide an explanation for your small size and dusky complexion. Also, the peculiar system by which the children of foreign princes and counts become princes and counts themselves, without regard for primogeniture, is ample justification for appropriating a handle of some kind. Count or baron is the easiest, and the smarter resorts of the world crawl with them. Maharaja is reasonable but a little more dangerous, since many of them are descended from God, and Indians, devoutly religious, may know their pantheon sufficiently well to rumble you.

If you consider a title out of keeping with the times in which we live, a change of name is simple. Beware of over-egging the cake, however. Windsor is unsound; people may think you are German or Greek. Guinness is likewise problematical because you will be expected to be not only Irish but extremely rich. The best bet is probably semi-consonantal substitution as in the well-known Smith-Smyth transition. An often used further step derived from Scandinavian practice is the *hyphenated patronymic* which can be combined with semi-consonantal substitution to produce splendid results: thus if your father's name is plain David Smith, you would be foolish not to call yourself Davidson-Smyth, legitimizing this by deed poll if you feel the need. A sensitive ear is, of course, a prerequisite. I have met few sadder cases than a fellow I came across in a very seedy drinking club who expected me to believe that he had been christened Darrenson-Stybbs and owned large estates in North Wales.

(ii) *Preparatory school without tears*   Since very few people remember anything about their preparatory schools, it is not at all difficult to manufacture a career there. The Gabbitas Thring Education Trust dispenses information to any who ask. Once you have found a reputable school, attend a sports day and wander in a nostalgic manner around the premises. In the dining hall you will find large wooden panels bearing the names of old boys. Find a name similar to your own, then repair to the school library and check its progress in back numbers of the school magazine. Then go home and write to the old boys' association secretary, signing your letter with the name you have gathered from the notice board, and telling him that you would like your copy of the magazine sent to your new address (which will be your usual leather-goods shop in Praed Street). From the magazine you should be able to pick up the rudiments of the school's customs as well as a good smattering of its secret language. It will also excite admiration if left casually on your coffee table beside copies of *Country Life, Interiors* and *Melons International*.

(iii) *Public schools*   It is generally more difficult to acquire a public school education without having attended a public school, as your 'comrades' may have more vivid memories of adolescence than of childhood. There is, however, a psychological technique which can, with correct use, ensure acceptance.

Start by using the basic research methods that made you a valued pupil-after-the-fact at your preparatory school. But this time, make quite certain that your *alter ego* is either dead or has emigrated. (How you acquire this information is your own business. If you have got this far in the book, it should be child's play.) Again, establish links with the old boys' association; strain every nerve to *meet the secretary*, who is almost bound to be a fellow who prides himself on never forgetting a face – and, of course, he will not recognize yours. He will, however, be embarrassed by this fact, because prospective old boys always get the benefit of the doubt: why should anyone try to muscle in on the Assoc.? *Unless he is a complete bounder.* And members of the Assoc. *cannot by definition be bounders.* On coming into contact with the cove, whom you will recognize from the many photographs in which such secretaries delight in appearing, you will use the 'Hello, old boy!' gambit. The best instance of this I have ever been privileged to witness took place in the smoking room of the RAC Club. The dramatis personae were the secretary of a famous old boys' association and Charlie Strangeways (*né* Maurice Clegg), a washing machine salesman on a self-improvement bent, not a member of the RAC Club but not about to let that stop him.

Strangeways: Hello, old boy!

Secretary. Hello. Um . . . Face familiar, can't put my finger on the, um . . .

Strangeways: Name. Strangeways. Gosh, it's a long time.

Secretary: Yes, yes, indeed. Um army, was it . . . ?

Strangeways: School. Hear you're the Hon. Sec. nowadays and doing a pretty fantastic job. Of course, after that goal in the house side final, one expects nothing else.

Secretary: Too kind, too kind. (*Muses*) It's coming back. You would have been in Clarke's, no, Watson's, no, School House, no—

Strangeways: Pargeter's. I used to watch you practising from Jammy Window, after Farps on Wednesday.

Secretary: Farps. I see. Of course, they suppressed Farps in 1952—

Strangeways: After Unction. Yes. Horrible. How well one remembers your stand in Borkers.

Secretary (blushing): Well, one has always felt—

Strangeways: Responsible. Yes, it is people like you who make schools like ours great, I always think.

Secretary: How kind, how kind. Have a drink.

Strangeways: Don't mind if I do. (*They proceed to the*

bar.) Can I interest you in a nice twin tub hardly used, one old lady owner stank like a polecat—?

It is of course, sad that Strangeways destroyed the gambit by introducing the commercial note; I concluded afterwards that it was because he had never managed to evoke a sympathetic response in anybody without selling them something. But you will get the general gist.

The alternative technique is to gatecrash an old boys' dinner and if possible make a very boring speech afterwards (see Chapter 7). If this is impossible, lead the faction of sober spirits which votes the expulsion of Colonel Mauleverer, formerly Mauleverer Minimus, for drunkenness. The more tedious you are, the more likely everyone will be to realize that they knew you all the time but, well, hardly surprising one would have forgotten a man as tedious as that. I mean, I *mean*. . . .

QUALIFICATIONS

The end result of formal education is no longer, depressingly, a nodding acquaintance with the classics and the ability to hold one's own in a discussion about other people's cousins. Nobody is now considered to have an education until he has passed various exams and possesses the certificates to prove it. These certificates accompany him through life, much as the record card of a pig accompanies its subject from farrowing to slaughter.

At first sight, the passing of examinations, involving as it does application and a certain amount of intelligence, appears an insuperable hurdle to the self-educator. Further investigation, I'm pleased to report, shows that this is not the case.

GCSES AND ALL THAT

These are generally considered *de rigueur*, even in such bastions of ignorance as the City of London. The certificates are printed on thick paper white on one side and bearing a squiggly eau-de-nil background on the other, presumably to deter forgers. They are easily manufactured by anyone who is prepared to spend a few coppers experimenting with a colour xerox machine, a little glue and a borrowed original. (Rack your brains if any; you must know *someone* with a GCE pass.) It is also worth noting that the eau-de-nil colouring washes off with water, so the really parsimonious can use a plain paper black-and-white copier and explain it away with a tale about a disastrous flood or (better still) a capsize during a celebratory post-examination rowing race at Radley, Eton or Gordonstoun.

BA AND MA

These are also photocopiable. If you experience difficulty in getting hold of an original, acquire a manual typewriter and write yourself a postcard from the dean of degrees of your choice, to the effect that the dean is terribly sad that you decided against the fellowship offered you by the college but quite understands that one about to make such a tremendous mark on the world as you are should wish to enter public life without delay. Unfortunately the dean has run out of degree forms for the moment but he is sure that prospective employers will accept this postcard as a substitute until such time as he has some more printed.

They never check.

Bounder's Briefing

PROFESSIONAL QUALIFICATIONS

There are many fine institutions, mostly based in the United States of America, that bestow qualifications on payment of a small fee. These usually take the form of a certificate, suitable for framing, assuring the world that you meet the institution's requirements for a doctorate of religion or medicine, membership of an institute of chartered accountants or architects or engineers, and so on.

It is possible to acquire university degrees in the same way. This is not, however, a course of action I recommend. Oxford and Cambridge degrees are cheap and easy to make, and carry far more weight.

3
A Grifter's Guide to Graft

It was Count Charlie von Anschluss, an old and valued friend, who formed my own attitude to work. Charlie was a devout student of scripture, having in his youth spent three years collecting from door to door in aid of a mission of his own devising. 'Consider the lilies,' he used to say. 'They toil not, neither do they spin; and behold, Solomon in all his glory was not like unto one of those.'

He was a living example of what he preached. He had once met a fellow who worked at the printers producing the Eton College school list, and had by means he could not disclose persuaded this printer to incorporate his name in that immensely valuable document. Since the mothers of debutantes use the list as a source of eligible males, the invitations soon began pouring in. Charlie, a man of immense personal charm, rapidly found himself staying in one or other of the stately homes of England each weekend, his needs tended by a huge staff of servants. A tireless worker, he was on the point of marrying a Rothschild when another woman whom he had been unwise enough to marry a few years previously spoilt it all by claiming him as co-tenant of the Willow Tree, a roadhouse a few miles to the north of Hendon. Until this disaster, Charlie was a byword. I am always meaning to go and see him in the drying-out home, though somehow I never get around to it. You know how it is.

It always seems one of the most absurd hypocrisies of our time that while the things money can't buy are put forward as being the most valuable, it is seldom legal to enhance the value of things money *can* buy by getting them without paying for them. If you have acquired an education along the lines I have already described, however, you should be on fairly easy terms with the legal system and ready to absorb some wisdom about making a living.

THE OBJECTS OF WORK

Most people in what now passes for society work because they can't think of anything better to do. (I have always been amazed that people seem so *upset* about being unemployed; personally I can think of few more delightful states.) They seek abstract concepts such as job satisfaction, spending hours daily in hostile, artificially lit environments. It is the sense of *usefulness* that one finds so repellent. Occasionally they may claim that they are not being paid enough and strike as a result, thereby losing several weeks' pay for the sake of a principle.

Principles have no part to play in the working life. The only purpose of work is to earn maximum money with minimum effort in the most agreeable possible surroundings. The only advantage of principles is that other people have them, thereby making life easier for those who do not. For those who at the sight or smell of a principle feel physically nauseated, there are several professions in which they are a positive hindrance.

My own experience reflects this. After an unfortunate crisis in the affairs of Chance Manhattan, my first banking enterprise, I was forced to find employment under an assumed name at Catford Used Vauxhalls. Catford Used Vauxhalls was an enterprise started by Charlie Farquhar after a nasty brush with

the stewards at Catterick. Charlie stopped being a
jockey (he was a small man, which may be the reason he
was known to many as That Little Farquhar) and
chanced to buy a Ford Zephyr at a lot in east London. It
goes almost without saying that the Zephyr shortly
afterwards ceased to function; Charlie pushed it round
the South Circular and down to Catford, where he sold
it. Charlie could sell anything, including his grandmother (twice). In time he expanded until full fifty
square yards of Catford High Street (the Bromley end)
hummed with activity. It became to the used car trade
what 52nd Street became to the jazz world – a mart
where great artists whose genius was unrecognized or
in eclipse could gather and recuperate before setting
out into the world again.

When I went to work there, friends clicked their
tongues and tended to view me with pity. Not a bit of it:
after the foul cloud of rectitude and public-spiritedness
hovering over the deliberations of the Securities and
Exchange Commission, Catford was like a pure
Mediterranean breeze. This was the forest primeval,
and one felt thoroughly at home.

I am often asked *why it is necessary to have a job at*

all. At its most basic level, the reason is simple. Unless you appear to have worked for a year or two, you do not get any payments whatsoever from the Department of Social Security. Although these payments are exiguous (unless you have a wife and several children, in which case I do not feel you are qualified to read this book), they do pay for, say, a tie or a pair of socks every week.

70

In addition, the arrival of a cheque in a bank account now and then qualifies you for *credit*, perhaps the most important stepping stone for the bachelor bounder (see Chapter 4).

GETTING AHEAD IN THE WORKPLACE

The depressing truth of the matter is that at some time in his life just about everybody has to make the pilgrimage through hideously crowded streets to a dreary room in which he will shuffle bits of paper round a desk all day. Personally I find this phase of my life almost too depressing to contemplate. But on rereading copies of the file on Chance, H., which I extracted from the personnel manager's office, many pleasurable memories filter back. (Not least of these is of the thighs, creamy above black stocking tops, of Miss Rudge, the personnel manager's secretary, with whom I was forced to fornicate on the blotter in order to gain access to the key.)

I see that I have already hinted at two of the gambits required for success in the office, namely File Substitution and Creative Fornication. These are merely part of the grand strategy, which can best be outlined under two heads:

(i) How to let others do the work
(ii) How to let others take the blame

HOW TO LET OTHERS DO THE WORK

Probably the only time in my life when I have ever made a good resolution was in the taxicab in which I was approaching the Occidental Jute Bank, Mincing Lane, scene of my first and only formal employment. I resolved to knuckle down, set to and graft away, in order to learn things that might later be useful to a czar of finance. The resolution lasted twelve minutes and five seconds by my Rolex – long enough for a dreary-looking chief clerk to usher me to a desk, give me a ledger to copy, and disappear. After this a seedy individual at the next desk leaned over and offered to do my work as well as his own for one and threepence an hour. Since this represented a clear profit to me of one shilling, I naturally concurred.

The seedy man's name was Price. It was a full week before I realized that if we were apprehended, he as well

as I would be sacked. After that I retained my salary in full and he worked on in mortal fear of exposure. His submissive attitude was entirely due, as he told me one day when I had made him drunk for some purpose that I cannot now recall, to my ease of manner and crispness of attire – he thought it impossible that I was doing the job for money, and therefore jumped to the conclusion that I had less to lose than he.

Unfortunately the burgeoning of the trade union movement and the death from overwork of a generation of drones has largely removed the Prices from the scheme of things. But the principle still holds good. Neatness of dress, with some (but not too much) attention to fashion; jauntiness of manner, with frequent references to exotic behaviour outside working hours; and, of course, the patina applied to the personality by a careful education – these are the factors that wither and shrivel your fellow workers.

Starting in the mailroom
The mailroom is a popular base camp for approaching the heights. A reasonable supply of smutty stories will get you the post of mailroom jester, enabling you to

recline on a pile of registered letters sipping tea while others wrestle with brown paper and sticky tape. If anyone actually asks you to handle any mail, take it to some quiet place and dispose of it. The River Thames is ideal. Even your slow-witted workmates will soon realize that you will shortly be sacked or promoted; and since your manner and dress preclude sacking, promotion is clearly the only avenue. If you are not confident about your manner and dress, scout around the office for embarrassing secrets, hiring a private detective if necessary. A file of the marital or financial misdeeds of your superiors will be extremely persuasive in a dark hour. Sharing the file will also win you influential friends.

Clerical grades

A terrible dustbin for all that is most stunted in human aspiration, normally filled to bursting with the rejects of the mailroom. Allow your pen to travel briskly over whatever paper is placed in front of you until you have sized up your workmates. One of them will be working far harder than anyone else, remaining at his desk long after the pubs have opened in the hope that he will be earmarked for promotion. Befriend him, asking his advice on knotty points of form-filling. At the same time imply that you are a protégé of the managing director and often share a game of billiards at the club. Soon this pitiful plough-horse will be seizing paper from your desk and processing it with flecks of spittle rampant on his chin, convinced that recognition will funnel down from above, with you as the conduit.

During any time that you can spare from the public house or betting shop, prepare an analysis of the department and send it to someone higher up in the organization. Use your assets; deviousness and cynicism are powerful management tools. Your superiors will be amazed by your grasp and understanding. Present your hardworking friend as the lynchpin who should under no circumstances be moved. You will almost certainly be swiftly promoted; any chagrin the lynchpin may feel can be offset by arranging to have him moved close to a window or on to a carpet, should your heart soften to this extent. It will make him grateful without turning him into a threat. You will also be able to use his undoubted industriousness for your own purposes when you are dodging hard labour in years to come.

The executive ladder: lower rungs

Here the game changes. Hitherto, you have been avoiding dull, repetitive tasks. From now on you will be avoiding *decision-making*, a manoeuvre calling for a high level of skill. The traditional method of breeding up a decision-maker is to give him to an existing executive as an assistant. These chaps can be tricky, if young; their jaws move remorselessly over their nicotine chewing gum, their eye is steely and misses little, and they are so boring as to be almost impossible to talk to. If old, however, they have normally fallen victim to what is called the Peter Principle, being promoted one step above their level of competence, and then relapsed into a pleasingly stagnant backwater. These charming old buffers like nothing more than to sip whisky before eleven and dispense wisdom afterwards. Nod wisely, plotting the while. Get your friend the workhorse in junior clerical to submit to you his long-meditated plan for reorganization of the department in which you are now working. Present it to your old buffer; he will reject it. Rewrite it yourself, signing it with the buffer's name; he will accept it. Put the word about that it was you, not the old buffer (and *certainly* not the workhorse) who originated it; you will be promoted.

The beauty of this particular scheme is that the reorganization you propose is *completely irrelevant*. If, for instance, you work in a toothbrush manufactory, it should concern some methods of critical path supervision assessment from head stamping to bristle implantation. Get a department with a title like that and nobody will have the nerve to ask what the hell you are up to.

The executive ladder: teetering at the top

No matter how confident you may feel about your destiny, the moment at which the ageing executive disappears is a shaky one. Hitherto you have pursued the time-honoured avocations of parasite and sycophant. Now you will have to make your own waves. If you find yourself at a complete loss, change jobs; your curriculum vitae will by now possess many of the glories of the Bayeux tapestry, and irrelevant billets are easy to find. Unfortunately, by chickening out at this stage you will forfeit the name of bounder, becoming instead a mere time-server. A better move is to reach for the nearest management manual, absorb its wisdom, and start hiring people. Hire only the young and talented; they will thrash around creating their own work, and their success will reflect well on you, their head of department. Any women you hire need not be clever. Surely you do not need me to tell you that it is more important to be surrounded by dim-witted beautiful women you have engaged at salaries far above their level of intelligence than by industrious frumps.

By the time you have reached the top, you will not be inclined to take any advice but that of your lawyer and accountant; I shall therefore offer no more. If, however, insecurity still nags at the breast of your impeccable pinstripe waistcoat, you may find some useful tips in the section below. My own dignity, reserve and personal charm have made it unnecessary to use this advice; but I have observed its effect and unfortunately one cannot choose one's readers.

HOW TO LET OTHERS GET THE BLAME
However well regulated your career, you may find that there are moments when your sophisticated approach

produces results which may be misunderstood by your superiors. It is at this point that many people experience disciplinary action. Some masochists derive a perverse satisfaction from this confirmation of their sense of guilt. Those who do not possess a sense of guilt, among whom must be numbered anyone likely to benefit from my advice, find the process tedious. Luckily, there are well-established procedures for sidestepping the unpleasantness consequent on such misunderstandings. They do, however, demand application, since short-term solutions to such problems may simply be seen as excuses, tactically useful but strategically unsound.

Ducking

A chap I met in the army told me that during the war he was standing in the queue to loot the spirit supply of a café when he chanced to bend down to tie his bootlace. At this point a sniper's bullet whizzed over his head and splattered the man behind him. The chap said that it was the happiest moment of his life, and one can see his point.

Thus, when something goes wrong, *keep your head down*. If the chairman rings up and asks you why the

Consolidated Albumen contract was never signed and what you propose to do about explaining the loss of two point five million quid to some irritable shareholders, tell him that you are too busy to discuss the matter since you are in the middle of negotiating a five-point-four-million-quid deal with Amalgamated Urea. He will keep searching until he finds someone who appears to know something about Consolidated Albumen, and will purge his ire by firing that person. With any luck, by the time Amalgamated Urea goes down the tube, he will have forgotten the whole business. Never duck merely to avoid being hit; the people up there are not looking for the facts of the matter, but for a victim.

If by some disagreeable chain of circumstances you find that you are saddled with the blame, hastily find a book on pre-Raphaelite art and make a study of Holman Hunt's painting *The Scapegoat*. Note particularly the expression on the face. Adjusting your features as closely as possible to those of the blighted animal, offer your resignation, stating that while the whole beastly business was due to the incompetence of Smith, Carruthers and Robinson, you understand that they as family men need their jobs more than you.

Real managers realize the irrelevance of family life; as well as getting shot of Smith, Carruthers and Robinson, who have probably been making themselves awkward for some time by showing people photographs of their children, you will probably achieve an increase in salary.

Illness

Nothing is more impressive than the sight of an executive soldiering on while his body falls to pieces. Discreet publicity will help: ulcer medication such as Maalox can be displayed on a shelf or surface behind your desk, as can nitroglycerine pills. Five minutes spent at nine o'clock every day with the head buried in the hands and a certain amount of muffled groaning serve to excite pity and terror. A man I once knew rose to be managing director of a publicly quoted company simply because he had mounted on the wall of his office a case containing a syringe filled with digitalis and marked 'IN EMERGENCY BREAK GLASS'.

Managements are notoriously reluctant to fire a victim of chronic illness, preferring either to shift the blame on to healthier shoulders or to push the sufferer

into a less demanding but equally well-paid job.
Diseases should, however, be carefully chosen.

Impressive Diseases	*Personnel Director's Note*
Heart conditions Ulcers	Stress-created: poor chap works too hard
Parkinson's disease Multiple sclerosis Sudden fractures	Jolly bad luck
Leprosy Green Monkey fever	Extremely rare. Once worked with Albert Schweitzer, y'know
War wound	Feller's in ghastly pain all the time, of course. All right one minute, the next … bam! Of course he drinks to numb it. Wouldn't you?
Unimpressive Diseases	*Personnel Director's Notes*
Venereal diseases Cirrhosis of the liver Heroin addiction	Been asking for it for years

Common cold	Lily-livered spineless dwarf
Slight sprains	
Alcoholism*	May at any moment vomit in the out tray
Schizophrenia	Had it for years, obviously. Lucky he didn't kill us all

All diseases work best if reported by third parties. Failing a third party, put two marbles in your mouth, ring up the personnel director claiming to be Dr Hector Moriarty of Wimpole Street, and give him the sad facts of your case.

Forgery

Much if not all work is tedious. It is, therefore, not surprising that the majority of blame-attracting misdeeds are sins of omission, usually involving letters or memos. A steady contribution of strong drink to the mailroom can reduce its efficiency to a level where nothing is surprising and nothing, thus, your fault. If, however, there is a teetotaller wreaking havoc there,

* Except in Fleet Street.

sterner measures are required. Faced with an unsent letter and a stream of vituperation, the cunning operative merely types a carbon, inserts it in the file, and sticks to his story like a limpet. *Anything* can be forged, and usually is.

Thumb in the dyke

An absolute winner, known by some as the Reversed Scapegoat, this is so astonishingly effective that I am in two minds about revealing it. It brings into play the purity of Sir Galahad combined with a flowering of the public-school spirit of the type popularized by *Tom Brown's Schooldays*. (It is no good in multi-nationals and other organizations with the corporate togetherness of a shoal of piranha fish.)

When the memos about errors begin falling on your desk, send one back to the effect that you are conducting a full investigation with the help of the local Fraud Squad. Do not, of course, call in the Fraud Squad. Take it easy for a week or so; then send another short memo, as tight-lipped as you like, to the effect that you have reached the bottom of the problem, which originates from a lack of communication within your personal management structure; this problem was really nothing to do with you, the communications system having been set up by your predecessor. Also, the person responsible is having serious recurrent personal difficulties. This notwithstanding, *you are of course obliged to accept full responsibility and tender your resignation as of today.*

To my knowledge, nobody who has used this gambit has *ever* been fired. Eighty-one per cent have received immediate promotion, with all that that implies.

It is always worth firing one of your subordinates at random a couple of weeks later just in case anybody up there does any real detective work.

The foregoing should be an insult to your intelligence, since nobody with a brain in his head needs a job at all. I am for the moment prepared to give you the benefit of the doubt, however; offices are undoubtedly useful places. Copying machines, postage stamps, telephones and secretarial services help form a large part of the independent operator's overheads, and it is always agreeable to find someone who provides them free. I personally light daily candles for the financial health of various public corporations which have provided me with these facilities in the past. At least I do when I am in a Roman Catholic church, which, of course, is very seldom.

There are few more welcoming sounds that that of an office duplicating room in full swing; the hum of the machine, the gurgle of the whisky bottles, the squeaks of goosed secretaries and the rumble of conversation about racing. Ah, the ever-open cash boxes of Dixons! The endless stream of email between Ladbrokes and Morgan Grenfell! The sweet moans and luscious breasts of typists at the DSS! But I digress and am in danger of becoming seedy.

THE PROFESSIONS

Since bounders as a rule do not take kindly to work, they make poor professionals. Either they rub along in the lower echelons or they cease to bound with anything resembling adequacy. But there are certain selected walks of life which seem created by Divine Providence to fit the aptitudes of the bounder. The central requirement is that they should demonstrate the alchemical transmutation of the bounder's natural inclinations into power, money, or both. There are other requirements, which experience has enabled me to systematize into the three questions below:

A. Does this profession require a marked degree of honesty?
B. Will this profession make me very, very rich?
C. Can I carry out this profession drunk as well as sober?

Rate the answers to these questions on a scale of 0 (No) to 10 (Yes). Subtract your score for question A from the combined scores of B and C to arrive at the Chance Rating. Any profession showing a Chance Rating of +15 or above is definitely worth considering. Take, for example, politics:

A	0
B	10
C	10
Total	20 points

Excellent.

POLITICS (chance rating: 20)

Whatever the Labour Party may say, in order to succeed in politics in this country, you have to persuade people to vote for you. This operates in the Under-Twelves Debating Society as well as in the Cabinet, and is usually achieved by barefaced lying sweetened with certain techniques (see below).

(i) *Getting selected* First, choose your political party. It does not much matter which; the only prerequisite is to stick to your choice for at least five years. The traditional route is to get on to the bar committee of the Young Conservative (or Labour, or Liberal) dance, and dispense free drinks with an unstinting hand to local constituency bigshots. Show a simple-minded dedication to party principles. Try to see everything in black and white, and say so, loudly. Selection committees are incredibly stupid and easily confused by subtle shades of opinion. Save subtlety for back-stabbing; stab hard, and stab often.

(ii) *Getting elected* Start your campaign by making a speech in which you promise all who attend everything they have ever dreamed of having. If it strikes you as being a popular notion to abolish all taxes and tow the British Isles down to the latitude of Madrid, say so. Senior party figures will be delighted to back you up to the hilt at subsequent meetings. If challenged by opponents, use one of three techniques:

(a) Make them look foolish by asserting that their short-sighted policies and these policies alone have doomed Britain to heavy taxation and its present chilly location in the temperate zone.

(b) If confronted with a real poser, start talking about *anything but the subject matter of the question*. Thus, if you are asked what you intend to do about the five million unemployed, explain a few good knots for use on towropes.

(c) If you are really in trouble and you know you are going to have to put up some sort of answer, *rephrase the question*. For example, Mr Interlocutor may say, 'Mr Chance, in the light of geological testimony to the effect that the British Isles are not in the present state of technology capable of being towed one millimetre, would it not be fair to say that this whole scheme is a cynical vote-getter?' To which you must reply, *like a flash*, 'What you mean is that the current state of geology teaching in our primary schools is woefully inadequate. True, true, quite so,' and carry on with a closely reasoned analysis of this vital topic.

(iii) *The back benches* Once you have been elected, you will be able to drowse your life away as contentedly as any peon in faraway Mexico, awaking only for divisions and uproars. My friend Humphrey Plunkett-Montague (Con., Pinner east), attributes his present position on the front bench to hypnopaedia. Having slept through four successive administrations, the clichés of power are so deeply embedded in his unconscious that on one occasion he answered fourteen questions without waking up.

Too much slumber may interfere with one's alertness, however. In order to sidestep this, two techniques should be brought into play.

1 *The publicity fix* During the summer recess, make the discovery that the traffic lights at the corner of Eustace Avenue and Bakunin Drive in the heart of your constituency have been out of commission for a few hours. Call a press conference to suggest that this is the result of a deep-laid plot to undermine the very fabric of democracy. Demand the instant recall of Parliament, and talk at terrific length on radio and

television, which at that time of year will be delighted to give you the run of their excellent facilities.

2 *Specialist nagging* Become an authority on a subject dear to the tedious hearts and minds of the public, such as weather forecasting. Delve into the weather forecasting system, showing it to be clogged with bureaucrats, riddled with corruption, woefully inaccurate and so on. Point out that an unexpected rainstorm in Solihull could be of inestimable value to an unfriendly power. Mention microprocessors frequently.

While this is essentially a publicity fix gambit, it also bears strongly on defence capability. Defence is a department riddled with bounders, who well appreciate the veil of secrecy that falls over the deliberations. Interest in defence is a rapid route to the front bench.

(iv) *The front bench* Having weaselled your way to a position of power, you will undoubtedly be asked to be Minister of something, and if you are a truly talented back-stabber, question-evader and bigot you may even reach the highest office of all. At this point, two approaches lie open.

1 *The Saul of Tarsus* Economic questions are never worth pondering unless you know the answer before

you start. This is best achieved by divine revelation, or if no revelation is vouchsafed, by the espousal of a simple universal panacea for the complex ills of the body politic. It is an excellent solution if you are not too bright, as all you have to do is bellow the same meaningless catchphrases over and over again, claiming the while that any who disagree with you lack the desirable front-bench virtues of firmness and resolve. With constant repetition, such catchphrases can turn into a sort of national anthem, enabling you to accuse opponents of high treason. The 'Rev.' Ian Paisley's famous 'no surrender' technique is an excellent example.

2 *The retrospective justification* It can take several years for a politician to arrive on the front bench. During those years, he or she will have had to scrabble hard. In the course of the scrabbling he or she will undoubtedly have said some extremely stupid things which may also be mutually contradictory. These contradictions have a way of surfacing at awkward moments, like Question Time, and can be temporarily smoothed over by the methods discussed in 'Getting Elected'. But sooner or later some repulsive little

journalist is going to start asking how, and why, and would it be possible to have an explanation. At this point it is incumbent on the elected representative of the people to justify every single drunken, opportunist and corrupt decision as part of a coherent stream of policy dating from his or her earliest entry into politics. The policies of all major political parties have been formed by retrospective justification.

JOURNALISM
(Chance Rating: 10-20, depending on newspaper and job)
You will see from the Chance Rating that only half the jobs available in journalism are worth considering. Consistently high scores are yielded by working for the *Sun* and the gossip columns of the other tabloids. Although there is a school of thought that suggests that such work should not come under the heading of journalism at all, I differ strongly from this view. These men are only doing their jobs, and very difficult jobs they are. It is not everyone who can write insinuating sub-porn for a readership with an average vocabulary of three hundred words.

FINE ART DEALING (Chance Rating: 15-20)

The most socially acceptable form of scrap dealing, all of whose branches score high Chance Ratings. As with all scrap dealing, finesse is of the essence. There are three basic categories of fine art dealer:

1 *West Enders* These have showrooms that they call galleries, situated on or close to New Bond Street. A basic function of West Enders is to sell pictures which they have bought cheaply at extremely high prices, achieving this end by touching up any boring bits, engaging their clients in sexual intercourse and so on. A really talented West Ender may maintain a gallery for his own amusement and prestige while secretly pursuing a more lucrative trade in Italian religious art with the help of a few light-fingered friends. One of the tremendous advantages of this trade is that it brings one into regular touch with those of noble birth; furthermore, splendid blackmail opportunities can be provided by the smuggling out of the country of great works of art indispensable to the nation but not to their nobby, but impoverished, vendors.

2 *Auctioneers* A training ground for West Enders.

The advantages are largely social (see above), but can be enhanced with a little cunning. A fair gambit is to let it be known that your granny has forty Rembrandts, all of which she will sell via the auctioneer employing you if the auctioneer continues to employ you. This should ensure a life of dignified leisure in which you are fanned by Nubians during heatwaves and constantly supplied with hot toddies in cold weather.

It may be of use to repeat here the adage that while Christie's are gentlemen pretending to be auctioneers, Sotheby's are auctioneers pretending to be gentlemen. There again, it may not.

3 *Rural dealers* Outside the capital cities of the affluent world the tone becomes lower. Most civilized countries now have their quotas of drummers and runners. It is something of a moot point whether such activities are worthy of the attention of a bounder. My own view is that they most certainly are. Technique is largely a matter of personal initiative. Experience shows, however, that a clipped accent and the tie of a decent public school inspire confidence. Goatee beards, acrylic safari suits and open-toed sandals may be all

very well here in Aruba or in the snug bar at the Stolen
Whatnot, but they are a serious hindrance when you
are expressing doubts about the provenance of an
undoubted Fragonard at Scattercash Hall.

ESTATE AGENCY
(Chance Rating: London – 25; provinces – 25)
This occupation shares many of the characteristics of
fine art dealing. It gives limitless scope to anyone
possessed of a keen negotiator's brain, a flair for
language and the sort of ambition that does not flinch
at fleecing the desperate. The best kind of agency is the
one which looks after people's land as well as selling
houses. While the creative instincts can be satisfied by
describing Battersea power station as a desirable
residence in the Art Deco style suitable for a large
family and with extensive riverside views, the bank
balance can be filled with money skimmed from the
rents of the Duke of Shropshire, currently exiled in
Jersey.

Estate agency is also a useful profession for those
too timid for lying or larceny. Looking after a large

country estate in the absence of its proprietor imparts an agreeable sense of ownership. And, of course, there is no need actually to tell anyone you are an estate agent. A near neighbour of mine in Palm Beach once took a very beautiful Armenian woman on a tour of inspection of one of the estates in his care at harvest time, giving the impression of being the owner and proposing in the centre of the nine-acre. Overcome by the honey-coloured glow of the great house's stone and the gentle lowing of the surrounding rustics, she accepted. When she discovered the truth, she broke off the engagement, enabling my friend (who had already rummaged her astonishing physique) to sue her for breach of promise. A very satisfactory outcome, and typical of the sort of thing estate agents have come to accept as commonplace.

USED CARS (Chance Rating: 20)
Regarded by many as the ultimate training ground for any career (see my remarks on Catford Used Vauxhalls). The used car lots of the country are living proof that, contrary to the old adage, it is perfectly

possible to make a silk purse from a sow's ear (though, of course, the silk may not last very long; but what can you expect for that money?).

One is not suggesting that you dirty your hands by tinkering with the intestines of motor vehicles. The working classes are usually adept at this. At Catford I was able to profit from my years in Parkhurst, where I met Gillies McWhirter, a genius of the wrench. It was he who later demonstrated to me the amazing virtue of wrapping the pistons of an old banger in nylon stockings, producing high compression ratios for as much as twenty-five miles before dissolving without trace in the engine oil. His other speciality, no doubt a product of his Scottish ancestry, was to fill suspect gearboxes with uncooked oatmeal, thereby giving them the authentic 'reconditioned' feel so much sought after by our clients.

But even after the erks have worked their magic on the machinery, the task of the salesman is not easy. Years of experience and many a barroom tale of villainy have instilled dark suspicions in the general public. Your job is to allay those suspicions, close the deal, and change your address. Two basic techniques serve:

1 Always tell prospective customers that there is someone else interested. You would be astonished at the diseased Ford Zephyrs and Vauxhall Victors which have suddenly appeared more desirable than the Glass Coach under the influence of this gambit.

2 Logbook interpretation can be a clincher. Most logbooks show several owners, the most recent being a minicab fleet in Lewisham. It is up to you to persuade the prospective purchaser that this, in fact, means that the owner of the fleet registered the car on behalf of his grandmother who only used it during her yearly outing

from the convent of which she was mother superior. (This gambit is also useful in explaining away the ridiculously low mileage shown by milometers recklessly back-wound.)

After a year or so, you should be ready for anything. The usual test is whether you can sell for more than £500 a car which, due to its failure to start, has to be pushed off the lot by its new owner.

BOOKMAKING (Chance Rating: 15–18)

Not as popular as it once was, due to the emergence of large organizations headed by virtuoso bounders and backed by computers.

SELLING ARMS (Chance Rating: 20)

A classic profession, in which it is still possible to start small and villainous and finish big and political. It has the advantage of bringing one into contact with kindred spirits of all nationalities. Desirable qualifications include a short spell in the army, particularly if by adroit management of quartermaster's records you can leave Her Majesty's service with a couple of dozen assault rifles. It is unlikely that anybody with the political ambitions required of a good customer will come your way to begin with; but the growing *rapprochement* between armed robbery gangs and organizations like the Real IRA has made them part of the same large and eager market.

Nostalgic old-timers may mourn the departure from the international scene of towering figures like Basil Zaharoff. They should be ignored; enterprise and a sense of the fitness of things can still take you a very long way. In addition, weapons have become smaller and more portable. The price-to-weight ratio of an efficient tactical nuclear weapon would have made Zaharoff, accustomed as he was to dealing with Krupp monstrosities, drool.

The central problem with arms salesmanship is the high overhead. When you reach any appreciable size, you will have to pay off a variety of officials (remember Lockheed?) as well as maintaining a workmanlike private army for your own protection and as a selling tool. A good accountant, however, can make such matters count against your general tax liability.

Many excellent bounders have been deterred from the arms salesman's life by the mistake belief that weapons hurt. Nothing could be further from the truth. They help sustain the labouring classes of the manufacturing countries in the total comfort to which they have become accustomed. They are almost without exception destined for internal use only by the purchasing countries, which have a perfect right to maintain their citizens secure in their beds. And most important, since deals are normally made in some of the world's most comfortable hotels and holiday resorts, there is absolutely no danger to the salesman. Weapons are a very civilized business, whatever the inhabitants of Beirut may tell you.

MANAGEMENT OF ROCK-AND-ROLL ORCHESTRAS
(Chance Rating: 15–20)
This is a comparative newcomer and was at first viewed with scorn by some of my contemporaries. Wrongly, as I maintained then; and my observations have as usual been confirmed by subsequent events. Most Rock-and-Roll Orchestra managers of my acquaintance

are rotund, jovial fellows, sexually ambiguous, reeking of American whisky and unbelievably rich. What is more, their riches seldom seem to be founded on anything as vulgar as success.

It was once thought that a manager's job was to organize a band of hobbledehoys, find them musical instruments and transport, and share in their inevitable success. After the first few collapses from mental exhaustion brought on by poverty and driving many millions of miles in unsafe Ford Transit vans, the perception changed. Now it is generally recognized that while the world needs van drivers and small-scale financiers, they can be provided by the uneducated or the unwary. The entrepreneurial spirit in which we specialize is best expressed by weaselling the successful 0.001 per cent of Orchestras from under the noses of the rabble. I have heard this called theft, but prefer to think of it as a complex form of delegation.

Once you have discovered a useful Rock-and-Roll Orchestra, make arrangements to have large portions of its income diverted to you. Though this process is the foundation of any business enterprise, it is often difficult to make your victims understand its necessity.

The beauty of Rock-and-Roll Orchestras is that they are staffed exclusively by dope fiends who are under the impression that their cacophony is a form of art. This tends to blind them to money matters. If they do begin to get awkward, it is probably a sign that their stock of substances is running low, and it is up to you to drug them into submission with supplies acquired through your contacts.

FAILURE

If there is one thing I hate, it is unpleasantness. I would almost rather pay alimony to my third wife than face up to unpleasantness. Almost, but not quite.

But it is foolish to pretend that there is no such thing as unpleasantness; life is packed with the stuff, and if you turn away from it, it will strike you about the nape with a knotty club. I refer, of course, to the possibility that you may find that any or all of the above ventures do not produce the rich rewards and otiose style of life you expect. In short, that you will fail in your chosen walk.

Hellish, but there it is.

Possibly the most hellish part of it is that *you may not notice you are failing. Constant self-criticism is the essence* if you are to walk that knife-edge ridge between the twin gulfs of seediness and respectability. Below you will, therefore, find a list of danger signals.

RESPECTABILITY
You are in serious danger if you find yourself:
– paying any bill before or after you receive a final demand
– visiting any sick relation who is not rich
– doing anything out of the 'kindness of your heart'
– becoming interested in anything except drinking or making money *for its own sake*

SEEDINESS
Your standards are slipping if you:
– accept a job as secretary to a golf club
– are demoted by a bookmaker from bagman to tic-tac man
– become a private detective

– become a waiter
– marry for love
– frequent any drinking club not in St James's Street or Pall Mall, except on pressing business or to give instructions to your subordinates

4
Bounding Into the Bunce

It will not have escaped the astute reader that the main object of work is to provide a regular and copious supply of money. Since the international financial climate and the natural proclivities of the human organism make money difficult stuff to manage, I shall provide some hints on how to make what you have got, or claim to have, go a little further.

This is no place for a discussion of high finance. I have no intention of revealing the secret of my methods, except in exchange for substantial directors' fees. Besides, personal initiative and originality of approach are paramount in the world of big money. If you wish for further reading, you are recommended to follow the meteoric career of Chance Manhattan as reported by the *Financial Times* and the court record in the case of *Regina v. Chance and Others*.

What follows is in the nature of a few basic ground rules. Closely adhered to, they will provide a firm

launching pad for more complicated and devious schemes, not excluding advantageous matrimonial arrangements. The operative word is *credit*.

CREDIT – GENERAL REMARKS

One suspects that somewhere in the murk at the dawn of time, the cave man Ug may have found himself without a bone to gnaw, and, looking about him with his little simian eyes, have spotted Gak, with two bones. At this point he would have persuaded Gak to let him have one of the bones, promising to return it later, with an added lump of gristle as compensation for the interval of bone lack. Gak may have proved balky, claiming that both bones were necessary for his own security. Ug, however, must have pointed out that:

(i) by lending him a bone, Gak would provide evidence of his own magnanimity, and could gain kudos by pointing out to chance acquaintances the rippling muscles and sleekness of pelt derived by Ug from the bone's nutrition;

(ii) the lump of gristle added to the repaid bone would vastly enhance Gak's chances of acquiring a sixth wife;

(iii) he expected to be dismembering a mammoth of his own in a day or so or anyway as soon as his bad leg was a bit better. Also his rich bachelor uncle had recently been mauled by a sabre tooth tiger and gangrene was confidently expected.

Little has changed. Loans still add status to the lender, and make him richer. Expectation of enhanced status and wealth still lends weight to the feeblest excuses made by borrowers. Thus it was that within living memory no young gentleman considered himself worthy of the name unless he was being pursued by his tailor. The tailor, on the other hand, besides benefiting from the healthful exercise, had the satisfaction of seeing his produce displayed on the backs of the noblest in the land.

Recent developments have added sophistication; the principles, however, remain the same.

THE WEST END OF LONDON

There are certain establishments, particularly in Jermyn Street, St James's Street and Savile Row, where cash is very rarely seen, being regarded as vulgar (as indeed I have always found it). Their produce is extremely desirable, since it confers on the wearer a discreet cachet not achieved by wearing the stock of Marks & Spencer, Russell and Bromley or Burtons. It is, however, extremely expensive (and rightly so, since this makes it unavailable to every Tom, Dick or, come to that, Harry) and is therefore best acquired on credit.

If your father and grandfather bought their spats and boaters there, you will have no difficulty. But many who are understandably reticent about their parentage have discovered that it is not possible simply to stroll into New and Lingwood, purchase two dozen shirts and a Leander bow tie, and ask the assistant to put it on the account. This is usually because they do not have an account, and accounts are extremely difficult to open.

Old boys of the better public schools have a distinct advantage, as many of these shops maintain branches in the High Streets of nearby towns in the hope of addicting the young and impressionable to their merchandise. A friend of mine at Eton, observing that the tailors Welsh and Jeffries, the haberdashers New and Lingwood, the shoemakers Ganes and the bank Coutts lined Eton High Street, realized the advantage at the age of fifteen. Though he was at the school by virtue of a council assisted places scheme, he began what I have always regarded as the finest example of the slow build I have ever seen. Finally, impeccably shirted, suited, shod and overdrawn, he succeeded in marrying the daughter of a brewery magnate before her seventeenth birthday. His evasion of the bailiffs who lined the path to the church excited the intense professional admiration of his new father-in-law, previously a convoy escort commander in the Battle of the Atlantic.

THE SLOW BUILD

The only correct way of opening a non-hereditary account. (WARNING: like all feats of consummate craftsmanship, this may take a long time to mature.)

Select your target shop. Enter, fix your eye on the dimmest-looking assistant, and purchase a handkerchief, white, plain, linen, in a lordly manner. After a week, return, purchase the old boys' tie of an approved public school (see Appendix One) making a note of which one you have chosen. Purchase more cheap articles at seven-day intervals during the following year, always from the same assistant. After six months or so, let slip a remark about the weather, or a comment on the hero of a memorial service scheduled for noon at St James's Piccadilly. *Ignore the assistant's reply*. After a year, discover one day that you have come out without any money, and tell the assistant you will pay him next time you are in. He will agree. Pay him a week later. Repeat this operation at six-week intervals for some months. Then forget your money three times running. He will then suggest that you open an account. Open one. Pay the first bill, which will be small, and the next, which may be larger. (I realize this is a departure from principle but *il faut souffrir pour être beau*, as Racine – or was it Voltaire? – once said.) Wait until the manager goes on holiday. Compose your shopping list, which can be as long as you like. Now choose an assistant who does not know you. Then *stoop like a peregrine on its prey, purchasing all before you*, and tell the man to put it on your account.

This, as I say, is the traditional method. There are two others, which have come to us from across the

Atlantic. Like most American things, they have disadvantages: the first is very illegal, and the second demands a store of brass nerve inconsistent with true cowardice. But here they are.

THE FALSE NAME
This functions only with newly arrived or senile assistants, and requires a little research. Study the gossip columns until you find a mention of a peer,

preferably Scottish, who has not been seen outside his park gates since V-J Day. Visit the shop of your choice, open an account in his name and clear the racks.

N.B. Getting rumbled leads to imprisonment. One almost sure way of avoiding this is to *wear a kilt*. For some reason, no shop assistant is ever suspicious of anyone in a kilt. Of course, many would prefer jail, and who could blame them?

ON APPROVAL

Not strictly a method of getting credit, but none the less effective. Book a room – a suite, if possible – at the Savoy. Using the telephone provided, ring the shops you have scouted and arrange for a selection of clothing or other goods to be sent on approval. The shop, impressed by your address, will respond rapidly. The Savoy, seeing your room covered in packages from Turnbull and Asser, Lock, Lobb, and Fortnum, will revise its opinion of your credit-worthiness in an upwards direction. At least some of the clothes will fit.

How you escape from the hotel is your own business. A friend of mine packs a suitcase with crampons and a climbing rope down which he abseils to the embankment. My own preference is for a commissionnaire's uniform, a false moustache and the frontal approach.

CREDIT CARDS

There was a time when getting credit was an art unto itself. Either you were trustworthy or you were not; a man stood or fell by his reputation, or what he could persuade people about his reputation. Recent developments have chipped away at this important cement in the social fabric; every man, woman and child in the world is now bombarded with a confetti of little plastic cards with which, should they desire, they can live like sultans and potentates.

Since everyone knows just about everything there is to know about credit cards, I shall not delve too deeply into their vulgar mysteries. Suffice it to say that in my circle they are thought intensely déclassé. This is because they are so widely available that possessing one confers *no status at all*, whatever the companies which advertise them may have you believe. Perhaps they have their uses in buying Ford Cortinas, G-plan furniture, Royal William miniature commemorative plates, and the like. I neither know nor care. On the one occasion I have attempted to use one, I heard the sentence that has summed up my attitude to them ever since. It was old Milos Stugeron who said it to me, after an unfortunate evening at backgammon in Bermuda. 'If you think you are paying me twenty grand with that thing,' he quipped, 'you are out of your poxy little mind. You can stick it,' he continued, with that charming smile of his so full of precious metals, 'where the sun do not shine.' There was nothing to do except throw the thing away, put a brave face on it, and seduce his wife and eldest daughter (who, incidentally, later paid the debt when I showed her the memo I was intending to send the Earl she was on the point of marrying).

BANK LOANS
Everyone who was anyone once employed an agent whose task it was to underwrite any temporary cash-flow hiccups by selling a few acres of land here and there. Few of us now own enough land to make this

feasible; happily, however, it is no longer necessary, since the place of the agent has been filled by the bank manager. And while it might formerly have been mortifying to the landed gentleman to find that his deer park was unexpectedly the property of the Las Vegas Casino Club, the intelligent budgeter nowadays throws away his bank statements unopened and is not aggravated. Naturally, it is necessary to be on reasonable terms with your bank manager. But this is not difficult, since bank managers are almost invariably small men with powerful imaginations. Make them feel tall (a friend of mine conducts his negotiations via a circus midget); satisfy their wildest dreams (the midget arrives in a Rolls-Royce and is borne into the blond oak Star Chamber by matched Nubian giants clad in leopard skin).

Banks love lending people money. There is great satisfaction for the borrower in hearing the cheques land in the balance with the plop of a rock falling into deep water rather than the sproing of a pogo stick. And never, *never* worry about getting in too deep; the larger your overdraft, the richer the bank must think you are, and the more willing it will be to extend your facilities.

THE THREE TOUCHES

The central fact of bounding is that the bounder, entirely through his own efforts, moves in a social stratum where wealth is largely inherited. The possessors of inherited wealth find it impossible to imagine any acquaintance of theirs being in a moneyless state. The simplest and most effective means of obtaining credit is therefore to ask for it.

Bounding Into the Bunce

1 The touch direct

'I say, old boy, can you spare a monkey till next Tuesday?'

This depends for its success on your choice of touchee, who must be a man who habitually deals with sums of money that make £500 look a mere fleabite. Such people are not always easy to find, but a person of correct education, appearance and manner should have at lest ten listed in his address book. Parsed, this touch yields three significant elements: *old boy*, while an obsolete form of address, is class- and intelligence-specific and still carries tremendous force. The use of the word *monkey* for £500 has splendid sporting connotations calculated to enthuse all that is red-blooded in the ignorant plutocrat. And the specification of repayment date, as in *next Tuesday*, is reassuring. Undoubtedly, the correctly prepared touchee is led to think that next Tuesday is rent day on the toucher's vast estates in Derbyshire.

2 The touch circuitous

'Ghastly thing but I seem to have left my wallet in my other suit.'

Best used on occasions requiring postponed payment for goods, dinners or gambling debts (I need hardly say that postponement can be indefinite). This one functions on all social levels. It was of tremendous use during my time at Catford Used Vauxhalls, implying as it did that I possessed more than one suit. Used at Whites or Boodles and with the correct intonation, it can be made to imply that one's valet has omitted to make the transfer.

3 The touch plausible
'As a matter of fact my stockbroker's computer is on the blink; man says the cheque's in the mail but honestly one doesn't know who one can trust nowadays.'

A crisp functional touch for use with the newly rich and others who do not think it shameful to discuss financial matters in the social context. If you have a tiny account with a stockbroker, so much the better. Brandish the computer printout. Correctly chosen touchees will shudder, realizing that there but for fortune go they; the deep-seated human instinct to appease the blind gods of Chance will impel hands in the direction of notecases.

The real sting in this one lies in the tail: the careful reader will note that no repayment date is specified. Indeed, there is no guarantee that there is a cheque in the post. The more confused and thievish the operations of stockbrokers, the more effective the touch. And informed sources close to the City are confident that with time the touch can only gain in effectiveness. And of course, if you wear a reasonable tie (see Appendixes One and Two) and approach a rich arriviste or other yob, he will be positively flattered to fork out the loot.

ULTIMATE CREDIT

Laws are made by lawyers, and lawyers are stupid enough to have put in several years' hard labour to gain their qualifications. Laws made by stupid men need only be obeyed by other stupid men, and anyone who has read this far now has enough information at his disposal not to be stupid, unless he is completely stupid, in which case he will be too stupid to know the difference.

Unfortunately, some of the better methods of obtaining credit have become illegal and cannot be recommended. A Canadian friend of mine operated a near-miraculous system known as *kiting*, by which he borrowed money from one bank in the morning, immediately depositing it in another, leaving it on deposit for the ten minutes or so necessary for it to gain a day's interest, then moving it to another bank in time for it to gain a day's interest there, and so on. In this manner he was able to deposit the money ten times in a day, earning a day's interest every time, and paying to the original lender *only one day's interest on the overdraft*. Thus with an initial borrowing of $1,000,000 he was able to make a clear profit of $2000 a day (using, after a while, his own deposits as security for an increased overdraft). He used to describe it as the poor man's capitalism, and he was right. It does, however, demand considerable agility of mind, as my friend discovered the day he absentmindedly deposited his driving licence at the bank and gave a cheque for a million dollars to a policeman, who then refused to give it back. It is a matter of pride to us all that the words 'meteoric career' appeared no fewer than nine times in the judge's summing up.

Finally, always remember: a man's credit is as good as his reputation. So keep up appearances.

5
PAIR BOUNDING

MEETING AND DEALING WITH THE OPPOSITE SEX

An associate of mine at Chance Manhattan used to arrive in the boardroom with large black circles under his eyes and reeking of mixed Parisian scents. I did not have to inquire into the reasons for his exhausted appearance as one day he volunteered them to me. He had three mistresses, one a barmaid, one a debutante, and the last a nurse working the night shift. On leaving the office at four o'clock, he would dart round to the lodgings of the nurse, and serve her until eight. Then he would allow the debutante to buy him dinner, repair with her to his flat, and keep the springs creaking until her eleven o'clock curfew. At five past eleven he would collect the barmaid from some public house in Chelsea, go to her flat, and dally with her until four in the morning, and then return to his own bed having spent twelve hours engaged in more or less continuous fornication. When he came to see me he was in a pitiable condition, taking great gulps at a mixture of raw eggs and red peppers he had in a pint glass. He asked (as many do) my advice.

I told him that in my opinion his attitude was wrong. Congress had become an end in itself, whereas the skilled operative knows that it is only a means. The only one of his partners from whom he was getting anything worthwhile was the debutante, and even then it is little use being taken to Le Gavroche if all you can choke down is an omelette *saignant* and two dozen oysters while a lusty seventeen-year-old tears at your fly buttons (this is the last explicit reference I shall make to the sexual process). Give them all up, I said.

He must have looked upon me as a father – many have, although he, like most of them, had no justification. After I had made him drunk we went to a little spot where he lost ten thousand pounds at roulette (he was not to know I had a share in the game) and attempted to slash his wrists with one of those swizzle sticks with a little umbrella on the end. After I had dropped him at the hospital I visited the barmaid and left much later. Next morning he resigned from the

bank, already the wiser for his experience and my advice.

All of which goes to show that it is unwise to be too preoccupied with the opposite sex, unless there is something in it for you. And that it is even less wise to confide in anyone about your problems.

Why, then, are there two sexes at large in the world, and more importantly, why are they at it all the time?

1 *Procreation*   Said by some to be the best reason, since scientists claim that without it the West End would be practically deserted. As it involves hard work, expense, and court cases, I cannot really understand how it ever caught on. Whenever I see an eight-year-old girl I am convinced that Darwin had it all wrong.

2 *Getting ahead*   A much better reason. The story of Puss in Boots, who procured a princess for his boss by telling a series of outrageous lies, thus securing a lifetime's supply of fish, is but one of the many examples that spring to mind. Look, too, at Nell Gwynne. Not to mention Eduardo Pestalozzi, an enterprising young man who has just opened a chain of waterskiing schools after a mere three summers'

oiling the elderly at Gin Pins (known by some as Juan-les-Pins).

3 *Finance*   Eduardo again. And looking at the matter from a slightly different angle, many an up-and-coming young person has his or her first experience of top-level negotiation when persuading the parents of a petroleum heir that he or she only went to Alcatraz to get their PhD, and that homosexuality and heroin addiction need not present any impediment to a happy Baptist marriage.

4 *Pleasure*   Into this category comes love, which some say is a many-splendoured thing. This assertion is, however, not provable. Its effects are similar to those of a couple of bottles of champagne on an empty stomach, in that it makes its helpless victims intolerable to be with for others not under the influence, and leaves a nasty headache when it wears off. The fizz is cheaper. (In passing, I would point out that advantage can on occasion be gained from a feigned overindulgence in champagne. The same goes for love. It should not, therefore, be dismissed out of hand.)

THE ROLE OF WOMEN

We all owe a lot to women – few, since the Chance Manhattan Widows and Female Orphans Saving Scheme, as much as me. Indeed, the remarks above are addressed as much to women as to men. But women do face life burdened with powerful disadvantages. Medical science has shown that their tolerance for alcohol is less than that of chaps. Sexual intercourse may have long-lasting side effects that men are biologically equipped to sidestep. And whereas a man can make his way through life with a couple of the right ties and an account with a decent tailor, women are faced with the bewildering thrashings of the international fashion industry.

There have been some successes, it is true. But one generally finds that the female of the species is swept aside with the empty bottles at just about the moment when the serious dealing is getting under way. I have met only one exception to this rule, and frankly it is not a meeting the recollection of which is a comfort to me. In fact I shall be unable to bring myself to say anything about it unless my publisher makes it financially worth my while. Pending a satisfactory response to my demands, I shall leave it aside.

HOMOSEXUALS

Anyone who goes to a good public school will be able to cope with homosexuals, and will probably have gained considerable advantage from manipulating them. However, homosexuality is more or less a dead letter. It became immensely fashionable once it was removed from the law books, and therein lies the problem. On the one hand, it has lost its possibilities as a blackmail weapon; and on the other, there is seldom any financial advantage in a homosexual relationship, since there is no possibility of marriage settlements. The best that can be expected is a modest pension from an elderly admirer.

THE THREE PHASES OF A RELATIONSHIP

1 SEDUCTION: EASING IN

There are those who see seduction as the most fulfilling part of any relationship – among them, one supposes, the raccoon-eyed Don Juan of Chance Manhattan. They seldom make useful progress; seduction is a mere preliminary to the meat of the liaison. None the less, it should be approached with verve and conviction, following the principle that even the most skilled safecracker must first force his way into the building. The more poetically minded make the analogy with hunting. While this is an unpleasantly dangerous business (though associated with some decorative and prestigious clothing), one can see their point.

Choice of quarry is the first essential. It is unwise, if you are Jewish, to pursue near relations of any Saudi monarch (though you may yield gracefully if they pursue you). Similarly, it is foolish to be young and in possession of a red sports car and still expect much of the sixty-year-old Dowager Duchess of Shropshire.

Having selected an appropriate quarry, choose your ground. Most potential victims of seduction tend to be rich enough to move around a good deal, though this is not, of course, true of nuns. Victims with wonderful minds are often found in libraries of universities, but the best place of all to find victims is at parties; hence the need to keep the invitations rolling in, or at any rate to keep your finger on the pulse and the gates crashing about you (see p. 188).

Finally, choice of tactics must be carefully considered. Bounders of the male sex do, it is true, have a head start over normal human beings in that they present a challenge to the organizing instincts of the typical female. But it is unwise to place sole reliance on this. The wise will add to their repertoire the smooth tongue, expensive aftershave and heavy gold jewellery of the *creep*, another specialist species of the genus bounder.

Seduction is the blanket name given to the part of a relationship leading to the moment at which the object of your attention is first compromised. The compromise is usually, though not invariably, sexual. The means of luring the seducee this far is, of course, the major point of difficulty. Technique is a matter for individual preference. Simply as examples and not in any spirit of braggadocio, I have listed below a few interesting case histories. The protagonist could be anybody (though in fact, of course, he is me, and honestly it is difficult to think of anyone else in this country, if not the world, who can have had such success).

Points of technique

This is not the place for a discussion of the way of a man with a maid or vice versa. Those in doubt about this useful branch of interpersonal relations are referred to the works of Ovid, particularly the *Ars Amatoria*. If unable to read Latin, try *Pulling Birds* by Tugger Stubbs. One assumes that anyone interested in seduction for advancement will have the basic techniques pretty well mapped out; what follows is, therefore, in the nature of a master class.

(a) *The squashed dog* For this one needs a victim who has a dog. The object is to squash the animal, using a car. Wait until the victim takes his dog for a walk. Instruct your manservant or other accomplice (a taxi driver will do) to lie in wait in a car on the route. When the dog steps into the gutter to relieve itself, the manservant in the motorcar accelerates into action, squashing the dog. The seducer then rushes forward, shakes fist at disappearing vehicle, rings ambulance, fire brigade and clergy if desired, and offers consolation. Correct timing activates the phenomenon known to psychiatrists as transference, whereby the dog's proprietor transfers the affection felt for the animal to the first

consoling presence to appear subsequent to its demise.

NOTE: Dogs, while useful in all self-ingratiation procedures, should be handled with extreme care. The canine virtues of fidelity, generosity and rough good humour are at variance with those necessary for correct bounding. Dogs sense this, and may become violent, to the distress of their owners. A useful rule of thumb is never to kick a dog in a room with an open door, unless the dog is mute or you are confident of your ability to muffle its squeals with a cushion.

(b) *Closet heroism* It is surprising but true that the willowy, romantic type of person (particularly if female) is often hypnotized by violence. Violence is, of course, first cousin to pain, and is therefore to be shunned. The appearance of a violent past, however, is easy to assume and can be remarkably effective. Medals are easily secured in junk shops, although Victoria Crosses have become prohibitively expensive for any but fortune hunters prepared to sink a lot of capital into a really big pursuit project. An acquaintance of mine scoured a major coup by cleaning his fingernails with the pin of a DSO at a debutante cocktail party from which guardsmen in full uniform were shuffling home to sleep with their adjutants. In the same way, derelict heavyweight boxers can be hired and briefed to share with you loud reminiscences of the Big Yomp down there in the South Atlantic. Either of these gambits should produce wide-eyed, breathy attempts to elicit the truth. Refuse to be drawn. It is permissible to allow the eyes to film over slightly, as if gazing down hideous vistas of carnage. For those whose eyes do not film over readily, a slight limp in wet weather may hint at an old wound.

(c) *Power and glory*   Really busy men seldom have time for seducing. This makes them extremely desirable to women. Paradoxically, the appearance of extreme activity can be tremendously useful to those of us who are temporarily broke, and desirous of remedying the situation with a bit of hanky panky with the rich. An acquaintance of mine married a considerable fortune by telling his victim that such was his pressure of work that he could only manage to meet her between 12.15 and 12.20 a.m. at the tea stall on the Surrey side of Chelsea Bridge. During these five minutes he would never mention business, preferring instead to let the lights on the water and the romantic croaking of thirsty cabbies wreak their subtle magic. His home at the time was a railway arch in Southwark. He now farms twenty acres in Kensington.

(d) *Persistence*   Sometimes known as the Dripping Tap or the Chinese Water Torture, this technique demands taste, timing and an unlimited supply of gift vegetation. Having selected the object of your attentions, disguise yourself as a chauffeur and deliver her a bunch of red roses. Repeat the operation early every morning, leaving the card unsigned. Interest will develop rapidly; a sure sign of progress is the sound of a pleased gasp coming through the letter box. After a few weeks of this, the floribunda beds of the local park may be depleted. Abandon your chauffeur's disguise and deliver the bunch in person, announcing yourself as the sender as the door is opened. This is a critical point, as the chances are you will not measure up to her expectations or hopes. Bypass this as follows; ask her how she liked the diamond bracelet. When she asks what diamond bracelet, inform her of the diamond bracelet you concealed in a bunch two weeks ago. She will then turn pale and stammer, having long ago thrown the wretched flowers away. Tell her that you will go to the dump and rake over the debris. Choose a dump which is being filled in; pose against the bottomless banks of rubble, looking devil-may-care and holding a shovel if you must. By this time she will be racked with guilt and will agree to almost anything you suggest. On the way home, stop your taxi outside Garrard's and rush in. Make a quick circuit of the floor, removing from your sleeve the while the paste bangle you have previously secreted there. Rush back to the taxi, and fit it on her wrist. The toll gate is open; get motoring. . . .

(e) *Poor little rich girl*   There is no tougher nut than the victim who, on being taken to lunch at the Connaught, tennis at Wimbledon, tea at your club, the opera at Covent Garden and dinner at Le Gavroche, yawns in a feline manner and says not to bother to take her home as she has arranged for Daddy's chauffeur to collect her from the restaurant. It may have been Horace who observed to a bounder in a similar situation: *Fluvius cum mari certas*, meaning – as you, of course, know – that you, a river, are competing with an ocean. The only possibility here is a shift of ground, in order to make her feel guilty about her massive wealth. Simple squalor is ineffective, because it is boring. The vital factor is *squalor and art mingled* – always a mean combination. Take her to a terrible warehouse in Wapping, in which live pigs and motorcycles churn in gigantic vats of Dayglo emulsion paint. Introduce her to the flock of electronic composers you have lured to the premises with drink. Tell her that you realized as soon as you clapped eyes on her that she was the only really unique human being you had ever met, all others being dross. Monitor her progress, watching for signs of lowered resistance. At some point she will start buying drinks for the others, an excellent sign. Later, she will address Daddy's chauffeur as 'man'. This means that tidings of her new friends are on their way back to headquarters, and are a signal for rapid action. Take her home in a taxi, then have a man-to-man chat with the Daddy about the perils from which you have snatched her. If you do not hear wedding bells within the year, you are deaf. Or she may have run off with an electronic composer.

2 EXPLOITATION: EASING ON

It is sometimes difficult to gauge when a seduction is complete, particularly early in life, before one has become sensitive to the signs and portents. A rule of thumb is that a seduction is complete: *either* when the parents or guardians of the seducee are applying pressure for the relationship to be put on some sort of legal footing; *or* when the seducee, on bringing the seducer breakfast in bed, submits meekly to complaints about the incorrect consistency of the egg yolk. A chap I know who used to take photographs for *Vogue* regards his seduction as unfulfilled until the object has allowed him to eat two sizzling rashers directly from the skin of her bare belly. While this is theoretically excellent, my own preference is for fine bone china.

Once the seduction is satisfactorily accomplished a *relationship* ensues. Relationships are largely a matter of caring and sharing, ideally caring for oneself and sharing one's partner's financial resources. Members of a relationship normally live in the same house, and are exposed to two maxims: *nothing propinks like propinquity* and *familiarity breeds contempt*. Trite as these are, their message should be heeded – the former during the early, consolidatory stages, and the latter when the relationship is over the hump and travelling rapidly downhill. It is vital to be one jump ahead of your partner at all times. Thus, when the partner is approaching the top of the hill, you should be halfway down the far side and making appropriate plans with lawyers and financial advisers.

Twenty years ago, the legal status of a relationship was absolutely clear-cut. One married for money and fornicated for fun. If by chance one lived with a partner to whom one was not married, it came under the heading of long-term fornication, and when this ceased the assistance of lawyers was seldom necessary. Recently, however, life has been complicated by the LTR or Living Together Relationship, a device first manufactured by American lawyers for their personal enrichment. One cannot but admire them.

Bigamy, once used only by the desperate or absent-minded, is once again becoming fashionable as a result of the LTR (known in the UK as common law) phenomenon. This is because the collapse of a bigamous relationship usually results merely in a short jail sentence, whereas a common-law situation may render one liable for maintenance payments and public opprobrium.

Finance
As I have already implied, the only true object of marriage is financial advantage. Partners' parents should be influenced to yield up large gifts of cash or real estate in order to place you on a parallel footing with their offspring. Nepotism, whereby the financial gifts take the form of rapid promotion in the in-laws' company, should be encouraged, by threats if necessary. Since the invention of the industrial

tribunal, a sinecure so acquired need not terminate with the relationship. This, and the fact that capital transfer tax is not payable by nepotists, makes it one for the best methods of receiving the rich gifts.

Old hands always take their lawyers to meetings with their in-laws. Once this was seriously embarrassing, casting doubt on the intentions of the suitor and the integrity of the in-law. Micro-electronics have simplified the process beyond recognition. Go alone to the meeting, but go bugged. A small radio pick-up tuned to a receiver in your lawyer's office will relay the negotiations to his desk, and a bleeper on your belt will make it possible for him to interject sound advice if you are stupid enough to need it. Arrange a simple code if you are at all suspicious of the in-laws' integrity.

Aaron Spottiswoode, meeting the newspaper proprietor Lord Batley and bent on marriage to his daughter, was foolish enough to have his lawyer telephone him to the effect that he could afford to squeeze the old bastard harder about the house in Tenerife, because the old bastard had no use for it since he had given up the mistress he once kept there. Aaron took the call at the secretary's desk. On returning to the

Lord Batley

office, he deduced that Lord Batley had been listening on the extension from the fact that Lord Batley was threatening him with a revolver. The marriage which had been arranged did not take place. Further, Aaron told me later that until you have hidden for three hours on top of a lift in a newspaper building, you do not know the meaning of fear.

Pair Bounding

Once financial arrangements are on a sound footing, it is time to start stripping assets and salting them away in Switzerland or any of the other convenient shelters about which your advisers will no doubt be pleased to tell you.

Sex

No courtship is complete without sex. After the courtship is complete, however, sex loses its point and therefore its attraction. Continuing to take a strong interest in sex may entirely destroy a worthwhile relationship by fostering love and affection, neither of which has any place in marriage. This is not to say that self-denial has anything to recommend it, it is just that philandering outside marriage is generally recognized as being more pleasurable than so-called legitimate sex. And of course, legitimate sex had the disadvantage of being bound up with procreation, which, as we have already established, leads to overcrowding, litigation and other forms of human misery.

The family home

Choosing a correct partner, particularly for the first

time, will enable you to live in the style to which you have always wanted to become accustomed. As the entrepreneur in the partnership deal, it is your business to choose a good address. It is permissible for a single person to live almost anywhere, provided he has the support of an impressive accommodation address. Couples, however, are expected to entertain and, moreover, to entertain at home. In the unlikely event of your living in the country, address is not important, providing sufficient thought is given to the name of the house and the county you live in. Essex, for example, will not do. Street numbers are also obviously out of the question. Beware of tweeness; my first wife Enid, a charming girl who derived her huge fortune from her father's soap empire, wanted to call our little shooting box outside Weybridge En-Har Villa. It was with tremendous difficulty that I managed to persuade her to change the name to Chance Hall, at a stroke doubling my overdraft facilities, and ensuring that the noblest and best in the land first accepted my dinner invitations and only then began trying to find out who on earth I was.

London is easier, since the most appalling slums

have lately become desirable addresses – a good reflection on the initiative of estate agents, who, as I may have already mentioned, are no slouches at the bounding game. A word of warning: do not confuse trendiness with smartness. Belgravia and Mayfair are fine, as is Chelsea and, at a pinch, Fulham. Kensington contains some pleasant enclaves, though many balk at the prospect of barging their way through the throngs of Iranian students and other terrorists infesting the quarter. Regent's Park is reasonable. Anything east of Islington, however, is a nest of socialism ripe for razing, and should be avoided at all costs. South of the river is a howling desert. The sort of people with whom you wish to associate are unlikely to have heard of anywhere south of Battersea, and then they will feel they are taking severe risks with the majesty of their passports.

Entertaining

I have been married three times – first, as I have said, to Enid Catchpole; second to Phillida, daughter of Sir Carruthers Wymering, chairman of Chance Manhattan, deceased (suicide); and third to Louella Glutz, better

148

known as Désirée McKnight, of Hollywood. I think my marriages were just about average – a hot sticky courtship followed by a sun-drenched honeymoon; then bickering, financial machinations, adultery and separation. Elsewhere in this book I have expressed the opinion that my wives were lucky and lovely. They were, they were. They still are, if you like that sort of thing. But never did they look lovelier or think themselves luckier than when lit by candelabra winking in deeply polished mahogany, admiring my snowy linen and impeccable velvet bow tie as I laughingly prattled of this and that with the marchioness or screen idol on my right. In our entertaining, they found moments of true felicity. As indeed did I.

For the essence of every marriage is that it is an ongoing situation. And where better than at one's own table to formulate plans for the future? Gone is the necessity of running a courtship on furtive assignations in nightclubs and subtle inquiries of drunken bank managers. The Dior-smooth knee awaits the groping hand of the host. The handbag with its revealing cheque book stubs lies in the hall. The boards of the bedroom corridors have been certified creakproof by the host's own gimlet eye. . . .

Today's dinner guest is next year's bride.

3 REJECTION: EASING OUT

The naive, reading in the gossip columns that Freddie Worplesdon and Gloria (*née* Croesusberger), his wife, are divorcing, tend to believe in Gloria's breathy quote to the effect that Freddie and she, having grown apart, have decided in an adult and amicable manner to lead separate lives. When such a slice of information crosses the Chance breakfast table, however, there is a respectful hush. For I know the dogged work and relentless negotiation behind a press release of this kind.

One leaves school either because one's time is up or because one is expelled. Prison gates open, by law, when the prisoner has paid his debt to society. Even a job has its natural term. But marriage, if incorrectly handled, can drag on until the grave. It is the only part of life in which you are bound to control your own destiny. Fools can rush in, and fools can allow themselves to be carried on; but only the cunning can extricate themselves while retaining not only the shirts on their backs but also the significant portion of the spouse's jewellery and other assets.

A word of warning: if you have had children, there is very little that can be done. Indeed, it is surprising that you have been able to understand this book at all.

Bought off

Easily the best type of marriage is the one which never happens. I have been engaged nine times, and married only thrice. Two of my engagements have shown better project balance sheets than any of my marriages. This is because the parents of my intended, solicitous of their daughter's happiness, have deemed it meet to make it worth my while to withdraw my suit or, as one of them put it, to make me bugger off.

The qualification window for a buying-off type fiancée is small, as a friend who works for NASA once said. The girl herself should be extremely young, extremely stupid, an only child, and in the grip of some sort of craze. Roller disco was ideal, bringing lissom girls of the upper class into close proximity with acquisitive males of the *petit bourgeois* persuasion. Her parents should be extremely rich. As your acquaintance with the victim deepens, assure yourself that she does in fact fulfil the qualifications. Announce the engagement. Then send a letter to your prospective father-in-law to the effect that you are well known to be a mad gambler and petty thief as well as a homosexual prostitute, alcoholic and Ipsissimus in the local Satanist Trotskyite club. Sign it '*A well-wisher*'. When the dad taxes you, deny everything and arrange a personal confrontation. Convince him of the falsity of the allegations with a few well-chosen words. On withdrawing from his presence, take your handkerchief from your pocket and spill on to his office floor, or preferably desk, the torn-out 'Lonely Hearts' page of any well-known homosexual publication, with some of the more unusual advertisements circled in red felt-tip and marked '£25? Tops. Ring Tues.' As his eyes settle on this, burst into tears and tell him that his daughter is your last chance of going straight, and you are counting on him. Negotiations will then commence; if you settle for less than ten grand, you are a fool. The only flaw in this plan is the possibility that it was the prospective father-in-law who placed the advertisement in the homosexual publication, in which case flight is the only sensible option.

I have never used the above plan, of course. (A royalty of 10 per cent is none the less payable to the author on all successful gambits based on this advice.) One has one's reputation to consider. But you get the *principle* of the thing.

Untying the knot: you and the law

In Arabian circles, I am told, it is sufficient for the discontented spouse to repeat three times the words 'I divorce thee'. Western civilization has devised far more complicated methods, on the specious grounds that marriage not being something a chap should lightly undertake, it should not be lightly de-undertaken, either. Happily this monstrous piece of hypocrisy is now generally admitted to be a pious justification invented by lawyers to prolong court cases. 'Quickie' divorces are all the rage, and have made the lot of the bounder far easier than was previously the case.

In a split-up complicated by high finance or undue emotional involvement, the old ways are still the best ways. Pioneering American divorce lawyers have substituted for the old fee-per-hour system a percentage share of whatever they can screw out of the opposition, correctly concluding that clients will feel happier when represented by someone with equity in the extortion. One can only hope that this admirable system will spread rapidly.

Private detectives are also very useful, but tend to get bored if assigned to snoop on the same person for long periods of time. It is generally accepted that out of consideration for a detective's shoe leather, he can be presented with an affidavit of his employer's own composition for signature, the contents of the affidavit being anything the said employer deems fit to invent. Technically this is perjury, but there exists a good sprinkling of private detectives who realize that the ends justify the means, particularly if the ends are large cheques.

Untying the knot: you and your partner

Traditionally, the arrival at the nadir of a marriage is signalled by the departure of one or other of the couple, preceded by an outburst of violence and/or adultery. *Violence* is never to be recommended, as some women are extremely strong, and also unnervingly accurate with china and glassware. Clearly it is no good finding yourself a free man if you are flawed by the imprint of a Waterford vase across the delicate skin of your forehead.

Adultery is infinitely more pleasurable, but if you are the offending party the judge may think twice about giving you a share in the loot. *Non-consummation* is the only sensible route for Roman Catholics, but it does demand either a conspiracy of silence between the members of the partnership or a policy of total abstinence possible only to the dedicated or deviant.

On the whole *desertion* is the best bet, with the proviso that the deserting partner should carry off from the house everything that is not actually bolted to the structure. After desertion, it is advisable to change your name and/or leave the country until the hue and cry dies down. Jasper Hackett, with whose current wife I enjoy many cosy hours at his house in Aruba while he is absent on business, has terminated twelve marriages by what he calls his 'Around the World in Eighty Lays' policy. At the termination of each marriage you may (if quick) see him hastening towards the airport nearest his matrimonial home, clutching in one hand a suitcase stuffed with jewellery and negotiable securities, and in the other a first-class ticket to his next destination. The only hard-and-fast rule here is never to use the same country twice, and never to enter into matrimonial arrangements in a country you are also using as a tax shelter, as this can lead to the state of affairs pithily described by the French as the *nid enmerdé*.

DISASTER

I am happy to say that since my publisher has this morning responded to my demands for a further cheque, I am now in a position to reveal the truth about the only person who has ever worsted me. If the tale is unclear, it is because even now, as the palmettoes rustle before my verandah and the humming birds flit jewel-like among the breezeblocks of my condominium site on the quicksand, strong emotions stir like a dinosaur in the Eocene swamps spotting a newly dominant mammal.

Some years ago I found myself at a dinner party in Tite Street. The party was in aid of a Sunset Home development in Eastbourne which old Cuthbert Steggles was masterminding, and when I tell you that five of the eight males present were wearing Old Etonian socks with their dinner jackets, you will realize that this was a gathering of equals. The womenfolk were mostly familiar to me, some very. In a corner, however, leafing through Cuthbert's album of brochures with a puzzled frown on her heart-shaped face, there sat one I did not recognize. I approached her, and we fell into conversation. She was a distant cousin of Steggles, newly arrived from Arkansas. She had large green eyes and freckles and an air one could only describe as elfin. Normally, of course, one's gorge would have risen; but this time it stayed mysteriously put and made itself inconspicuous. Eva – for this was her name – prattled artlessly about the charitable intentions of Steggles, thereby revealing to me an IQ in the low 60s. I sat entranced, glass of whiskey untasted in hand. As the conversation proceeded, it transpired that her father, deceased, had owned an oil well, which was now in her own possession and part of whose proceeds were underwriting the Sunset Homes. By the time the butler announced dinner, I was experiencing a curious buzzing in my ears. From descriptions in popular songs, I recognized that I was in love.

After dinner we sat next to each other at the chemin de fer table. Eva laughed a pretty laugh and said she thought it was awfully clever of Steggles to deal off the bottom of the pack as well as the top. She could hardly deal off the top herself! Steggles tried hard to look as if he did not know what the hell she meant, but it was noticeable that he returned the stakes and then, at Eva's suggestion, the rest of his winnings and a little bit more besides. The evening broke up shortly afterwards, and I took her home. It was not until I was making cocoa, for which I had acquired a taste at Parkhurst, that it burst on me that I had simply let her out of the Jag in front of her flat without making any attempt on her person. I cursed myself bitterly, but without conviction.

Next morning I received a call from Steggles, who was offering to buy back a set of diamond studs which had disappeared from his dressing table during the previous evening. I denied all knowledge, pointing out that in view of his guests' proclivities it was a lapse not to have locked them in a safe. Then I rang Eva and asked her to lunch. She accepted over a line rendered indistinct by what I at first thought static and only later realized was the twittering of imaginary bluebirds. It is a measure of my mental state that I paid the bill with a cheque on a genuine bank account.

Later, as we were making our way to the Members' car park at the House of Commons where I store the Jag, she asked me where I thought she could get some diamonds reset. Acting on reflex, I offered to show them to an old friend who was generally acknowledged to be a world expert, and she readily assented. When I tipped out the brown envelope in front of my jeweller friend, I was astonished to find that the contents consisted of Steggle's studs. It was hard to believe that someone so ethereal as the translucent Eva should stoop so low. Then I saw the bright, nay, glittering side. To entrust me with her stolen goods, she must think of me as better than the general run of fellows. The nicked sparklers were as good as a love token. So it was that, with a tune on my lips and a song in my heart, I had paste replicas made, banked the real rocks and returned to her with a sorrowful countenance. I mean she could not be allowed to get off scot free. Her old man's oil well might or might not exist, after all. Tough about those false rocks, I commiserated, but consider the future. Side-by-side bounding, the double act, Darby and Joan swapping dubious stories round the banked but smouldering fires of youthful passion – was it not a beautiful picture?

Yes, she said, it was. She would be mine and willingly. But of course she would need the odd rag of clothing and this and that for throat, wrist and finger. Besotted, I tore through the West End like a simoom or harmattan, leaving behind me a confetti of cheques, none of them, this time, on existing bank accounts. Mannequins at the spring collections came to know us so well they would wave from the catwalks. At the sight of the red Jag seeking a parking spot, wine waiters would start hacking at the wires on bottles of Bollinger '66. Van Cleef and Arpels, Cartier, Garrard's poured a perpetual stream of packages into our suite at the Mayfair, all on approval and all approved.

The wedding was to take place at the fourteenth tee of the golf course at Wentworth, a setting which she found enchantingly English. The ceremony itself was modelled on the final moments of Elvis Presley's moving picture *Blue Hawaii*, with the King's College Chapel choir in attendance. Dressed in morning coat, Leander spats, a lei of pink gladioli, and lightly rouged against the ravages of the previous night's revels in Wardour Street, I stood waiting as the guests assembled. Through my mind flitted thoughts of the honeymoon, to be spent on Mustique until my lawyers had cleared up the financial aftermath of the courtship.

At this point, I became dimly aware of the put-put of a motorcycle engine. As it approached, I observed that it was a telegraph boy, carrying the familiar buff envelope. My best man stepped forward to take it, read it, and brushed reflectively at his moustache. 'Gawd strewth,' he said. Then, readjusting the mask, 'I think we should take a short walk.'

'Quite happy here,' I said. As a matter of fact, one felt none too steady on the pins.

He took me by the arm and led me into a nasty path of rough nearby. 'Bad news, I'm afraid.'

I read it. The words, as words will on such mornings, performed interpretive dances.

SUDDENLY REMEMBERED PREVIOUS ENGAGEMENT STOP
SAYONARA AND TA FOR SPARKLERS STOP SEE YOU IN FIVE
YEARS OR THERE AGAIN MAYBE NOT SIGNED EVA

I looked up at the best man. He was no longer there;
the prints of running feet led across the bunker and
into deep undergrowth.

'Hoy, chummy,' said a voice behind me. 'Would you
be Mr Harold Chance? Yes? Well, if you step down to
the station and answer a few questions about some
cheques and so on——'

'Do you carry a revolver, officer?' I said. 'One bullet
would suffice.'

'The British police force does not carry arms,' said
the officer. 'It is in my other suit.'

'In that case,' said I, 'lead on.'

During the following three years, four months and five
days before my release with full remission, I had ample
time to reflect on what had gone wrong. Two points
emerged.

1 I had met my Irene Adler, one of those women about

whom chaps write operas, and if I ever came across her again I was going to rent someone to make her ugly.

2 I had let the heart rule the head in a marital matter, and had therefore deserved all I got.

6
The Coward's Way In:
Bounding to Acceptability

Many readers may now be gnawing nervously at their fingernails and saying to themselves that it all seems very complicated and they do not know if they can measure up to the standard required. It may be all right for a man of the author's iron will and towering intellect, one seems to hear them mutter, but how can *I* ever aspire to such heights?

With difficulty, one is forced to say. But if it is any consolation, the heavy brainwork is over. All that remains is for me to give a résumé of the small touches which will put you in a position to begin, even if you lack the intellectual equipment to bound far.

Examined closely, the pictures of the painter Seurat dissolve into a lot of minute sploshes of brightly coloured paint. Viewed from a distance, the image becomes solid.

The aspiring bounder should keep Seurat in mind – not least because his daubs now command six and seven figures at auction. Mainly, though, it is because conveying a good impression is a matter of hundreds of tiny touches – tie, accent, make of car, colour of spats if worn, and so on. Unless you are one of nature's bounders the correct combination will not be achieved immediately. But in time, as your own style evolves, they will lose their unfamiliarity and provide a glittering carapace for the real you.

DRESS SENSE

Traditionally, bounders have been in the forefront of fashion. Suede shoes, for instance, were pioneered by bounders, who found that such footwear added a touch of distinction to the otherwise drab garments of the city dweller. The rule of thumb has always been to assume the protective colouring afforded by the conventions of the day, but to let the world know of one's exceptional qualities through a general briskening of the total effect.

450

Lock's →

← Belgravia Bags

Insignia →

← Balkan Sobranie

Old School (Variable) →

← Flag

Nourishment →

Snaffled →

Vaulting Ambition

Safe Seat

Permanent Loan →

← The Chase

If

↑ Foot on the Ground

THE BOUNDER

SUITS

The essence of the good suit is smartness. Tailors in Savile Row are excellent craftsmen, but they have a depressing tendency to produce garments which are so beautifully made as to be almost unnoticeable. There is obviously no point in laying out a thousand smackers for something over which the eye skids like a bald tyre on ice. An acceptable balance must be struck between the maker's label, which is found on the inside of the right-hand inner breast pocket, and the requirements of good taste. Good taste means a crisp shoulder line, broadened if required by padding; sleeves short enough to reveal the Rolex and the cufflinks, which should be ornate and if possible jewelled; the suit should be tight waisted (see also the section on corsetry); have a well-flared skirt to the jacket; and trousers tight enough to provide a seductive outline of genitalia (the legs flared or pegged according to the fashion of the day) is essential. Waistcoats should be worn fully buttoned.

A minimum of four suits are required. For city wear, *pinstripe* is more or less *de rigueur*. There has been a tendency of late for stripes to be worn so narrow as to be almost imperceptible. This is a mere vagary of fashion. Solid good sense dictates a bold stripe of a minimum thickness of 2mm, set at intervals of 20mm or wider and *running vertically* down jacket and trousers. Horizontal stripe orientation may produce accusations of poor taste.

For country wear, the *tweed suit* is essential. Once tweed was woven from brambles on to barbed wire, and its spines were capable of penetrating the thickest underwear. Physical agony forced many into wearing pinstripe suits in the country, leading to derision. Now, happily, synthetic fibres are used to weave tweeds which are not only kind to delicate skin but display a sheen somewhat like that of a starling's breast, and guaranteed to attract attention.

Evening dress, which once disguised the finest and most individualistic in the country as a rookery of penguins, has recently broadened its horizons. Once, the best that could be done was to sport black suede shoes in place of the regulation patent leather. These are still excellent, but can now be combined with a peacock array of silks, velvets and laces. Perhaps the smartest evening ensemble one has seen lately was that worn by Jack Goodenough at last year's Palm Beach

Realtors' Ball, consisting of a shawl-collar jacket in the Hunting Rubenstein tartan, lime-green acrylic trousers bearing thousands of tiny mauve replicas of Arnold Palmer's signature and wine-and-blueberry patent-leather co-respondent shoes.

Tropical wear, a vital part of the wardrobe, falls into two categories. First, there is the standard *ice-cream suit* for use by light sweaters of dark complexion, a guaranteed winner when worn with white kid shoes, fourteen-inch *puro* and panama hat. For those of fuller habit and pinker colouring, the *safari suit* is probably the answer, being short-sleeved, modern of aspect and occurring in a variety of delightful pastel shades. A bonus is that it is hard to suspect anyone wearing a safari suit of any deviousness.

While active sports are generally to be avoided, there are some which can be of use. Particular care should be paid to the state of the waistcoat if you are planning to play billiards. Paradoxically, smartness is a disadvantage here. A scruffy waistcoat will give the impression that you are new to the game, thereby making it easy for you to lose the first five games at a penny a point prior to sweeping all before you during the final game, played for ten guineas a point.

Other sports demand a tweed jacket and cavalry twill trousers. Do not be taken in by those who maintain that these should be baggy and well worn; they should be bandbox crisp, looking as if they have come straight off the rails at Moss Bros. Waistcoats should be custard yellow or Tattersall check, bearing the button of a well-known hunt.

SHIRTS

Stiff collars, formerly *de rigueur* for city wear, have happily disappeared. In their place have come one-piece garments, the body and sleeves boldly striped and the collar and cuffs a solid colour. Material, one need hardly say, should be heavy silk.

For the country, Tattersall checks are the only possibility. These are now available in exceptionally attractive colour combinations.

SHIRT NOTE: It is noticeable that many members of the aristocracy are either pop-eyed or scraggy. Those of base descent can simulate these characteristics by clever shirt selection. To pop the eyes, buy the shirts half an inch too small in the collar; to enhance a tendency to scragginess, an inch too big.

The Coward's Way In

SHOES

The question of shoes has exercised the minds of the fashion conscious ever since medieval monarchs proscribed the wearing of bells on the toes as too dashing to be consistent with correct religious observance. As I have already mentioned, bounders can be relied upon to give the world a lead. In the 1920s, they borrowed from the minstrel show the correspondent shoe, a wonderful confection in chocolate and cream, ideal for wear with white flannel or silk. Later came suede; and later still the elevator shoe, long the bounder's standby. This, like my old croupier friend Rafael Ortega, achieved recognition as the Cuban Heel. Now the wheel of fashion has turned again, and frankly just about anything goes.

For the purposes of business, I have always found that the wearing of brown shoes with the pinstripe suit hints at the larger freedoms and a refreshing defiance of convention. In the country, the brown shoes worn with tweed by the unimaginative seem unnecessarily sloppy, and may be thought to be camouflaging mud. Black shoes are not only conspicuously mudless, but hint at drive and crispness of resolve.

171

UNDERWEAR AND CORSETRY

Nobody who wears white underwear has ever achieved anything worthwhile. It is not always realized that underwear is worn to impress as well as to trap body heat. At its most impressive, it is printed with some suggestive motif such as zeppelins entering banks of cloud, firemen charging up ladders, female show jumpers negotiating obstacles, or (at the best and purest) scantily clad ladies of easy virtue engaged in certain acts. I need hardly say that silk is the only permissible material. A friend of mine claims in contradistinction that synthetic fibres, generating as they do quantities of static electricity, provide a continuous prickling of the intimate areas that aggravates the mind to great feats of graspingness. *Chacun à son goût*, but no, thank you.

Corsetry is the foundation of making a good impression. There are many types available through *Exchange and Mart*, the *News of the World*, and various shops which may also provide an accommodation address service. They soothe the hernia victim, flatten the stomach, square the shoulders, lift and separate and so on.

HATS

No doubt you too sighed with relief at the news that Guards officers in mufti were permitted to wear, instead of the bowler hat, the soft felt of acceptable cut. This pronouncement is symptomatic of the fact that hats no longer occupy the social mind as once they did. There used to be a hat for every occasion; in addition, sandwiches could be hidden inside them, and secrets kept under them. They could be stolen or shot at; policemen's hats were swiped with monotonous regularity every Boat Race night. What I am trying to say is, nobody would dream of leaving the house without the titfer.

Nowadays one needs only two – a grey and black top hat for use with the morning coat at Royal Ascot, and the sable felt from Lock for use at point-to-points or when impersonating an off-duty Guards officer (see above). My personal preference is to decorate the felt with a jaunty plume drawn from the Lady Amherst's pheasants at London Zoo.

In later years, when you move to warmer climes, you will doubtless shade your sensitive skin with a panama. Some consider this ageing. True, but it does provide a further site for the display of an old school ribbon.

TIES

A tie is not simply a means of filling the space between the top button of the waistcoat and the shirt collar. Any serious student of this book will by now appreciate that the tie is a poster, a personal file, a speaker of volumes. The knot should be either very large or very small. Those who earn their living by close work, such as billiards, may prefer the freedom of movement afforded by the bow tie – now available in most decent school colours (see Appendix One).

A word of warning: choose a tie that suits your complexion. An old Harrovian tie, navy blue with pairs of slender white stripes, should be avoided by those of Italian extraction as it provides a disagreeable echo for five o'clock shadow. Similarly, the distinctive shocking pink of a Leander's tie clashes unpleasantly with a nose that advertises its owner's conviviality.

SOCKS AND SPATS

Hosiery often presents the only opportunity for the peacock-like display that parvenu fashion designers would have us believe is the natural bent of the human male. While one wishes to have nothing to do with such people, it is undeniable that a certain amount of self-expression via the ankle is pleasant. As with shoes, a burst of rainbow clocking below the sober pinstripe trouser turnup can persuade the outside world that here is a man to be reckoned with. The rules respecting black silk socks with evening wear can be similarly bent.

Spats are considered *démodé* and non-functional. This is entirely wrong. Consider a moment: they are worn at occasions, such as weddings and funerals, when the tie is conventionally silvery or black respectively. The only way of impressing your *bona fides* upon the assembled company is to don a pair of old school spats.

A word of warning, however: the wearing of I Zingari spats at funerals, though undeniably lending an air of raffish festivity to the proceedings, may give offence to the bereaved. Unless this is your intention, leave them in the drawer.

HANDBAGS
Much in fashion with German and Italian bounders, handbags certainly do stop large objects distorting the

line of expensive suitings. However, since the only way
to answer the accusations of homosexuality attracted
by such bags is to thrash the accuser to within an inch
of his life, they are not recommended for wear by
cowards in the United Kingdom. Console yourself, as
your pockets bulge, that, while Jerry and Johnny
Petrolle may be nancing without let or hindrance, the
British Bulldog retains his teeth.

JEWELLERY
There is, in the British character, a quite ludicrous
prejudice against male jewellery. Unlike handbags, it
has a function – as an outward and visible sign of inner
and gigantic wealth. Reading from north to south,
permissible jewellery may be: the *tie pin* of gold, bearing
the flag, crest or motto in enamel and precious stones
of the organization of your choice; the *watch chain*,
from which may hang uncut diamonds, nuggets of gold
and heavy seals; the *cufflinks*, which should be large,
elaborate and colourful and may celebrate a casino or
type of car; the *identity bracelet*, in massy gold; the
watch, a Rolex Oyster, also in gold, and if required,

jewelled; the *rings*, signet, class and wedding; and (for the youthful) the *shoe chains*, preferably bearing the maker's name.

Earrings and neck medallions, though popular, are unsound. Having one's ears pierced probably causes pain; in the same way medallions, gold razor blades, drug cutlery, half ingots, shark's teeth, etc., may become entangled in chest hair.

All jewellery should be made from gold, or something that looks like it, such as highly polished brass.

PERSONAL APPEARANCE

While it is true that initial character assessments are based on clothes, ties, jewellery, etc., there comes a time in most relationships when participants look each other in the face. It is therefore worth spending a little time discussing the head, which at most times of the year is the only part of the body exposed to public scrutiny.

Many otherwise excellent bounders are let down by their faces. A lifetime of effort may have caused them to develop cunning eyes, a self-indulgent lower lip, etc. These are by no means fatal; plastic surgery is now simple and effective and, for those who are reluctant to undergo painful operations, there are more traditional aids.

MOUSTACHES

The traditional moustaches of the bounder are the *eyebrow* and the *toothbrush*. The toothbrush has unfortunately been discredited by A. Hitler, but the eyebrow still adds svelteness and distinction to an otherwise unprepossessing physiognomy. Those with large, rugby-football-shaped faces, which, when clean-shaven, seem to stretch in all directions to the horizon, find that the eyebrow underlines the nose, calling attention to its existence, which in turn leads scrutineers to the conclusion that those foxy little slots on either side of their ridge must be the eyes. Guards officers have known this for years.

There is a host of other moustache types, most of which need no introduction. The *Mexican*, obscuring the entire upper lip and a good deal of the lower, is excellent for those with weak mouths. It should, however, always be combed after meals. The *RAF* or *handlebar*, which joins the sideburns, is very popular with the middle-aged. I have often wondered whether its popularity with publicans is accounted for by the fact that it gives the gloomy an air of devil-may-care jollity, as if they have just bagged a brace of Huns before brekker and are on the point of telling you a good one about an actress and a bishop. The *Fu Manchu* has no place in bounding, since it looks foreign and in addition became a sort of uniform for the Provisional IRA during the 70s.

BEARDS

There was a time when the wearer of a beard was either deranged (George Bernard Shaw) or just plain scruffy (the Prophet Elijah). Happily, all this has changed and nowadays even traditionally clean-shaven professionals – take, for example, croupiers – sport the proud fungus on their chins. As with moustaches, choice of type is vital. The best types are:

YES   **NO**

(a) *Coarse pelt* A mat of hair approximately the length and texture of the outer covering of a tennis ball, extending from the cheekbones to the junction of neck and underjaw. This covers razor scars and acne, and also disguises facial chubbiness. Careful topiary makes it ideal for the concealment of a weak chin or pendulous jowls. Combined with dark glasses, it is also useful to those starting life afresh under an assumed name.

(b) *The goatee*   Worn short and pointed, this beard implies that the wearer is quirky, brilliant, proud of his chin, and almost exactly like D. H. Lawrence. This is ironic, as goatee wearers tend to be conventional, stupid, and generally have no chins to speak of. It is, however, a good beard for those past their first youth, provided it is not allowed to straggle like Uncle Sam's. Clipped to a point and waxed, it reorganizes a face rendered shambolic by the passing years.

HAIR

The hair of the bounder should be thick, long enough to bush out at the temples, and of a good colour. Youthful bounders will experience no trouble here unless they have red hair, in which case there is no hope for them, unless they resort to tinting and dying. By the age of about thirty, dark hair should be *greying at the temples*, a state of affairs that should be maintained with whatever cosmetic assistance seems necessary until the whole crop is naturally grey, at which point it should be allowed to grow out. Many grey-haired friends of mine prefer the distinction of pure white, which is readily achieved with any of the excellent preparations available at your chemist's shop. If necessary, explain the sudden transition by reference to a shock or grief too deep for words that has come upon you in the night.

The toupee, hairpiece, or 'rug' has always been a favourite with those who take a real interest in their appearance. They can be bought off the peg or made to measure. While off-the-peg models can given an interesting two-tone appearance, they do tend to excite ridicule. Made-to-measure rugs tend to be expensive, but match well. Renew them at frequent intervals, particularly if your natural hair is turning grey. If in doubt as to the match, ask yourself: would I buy a used car from the face in the shaving mirror? If the answer is no – and very few cars are sold by badgers with eyebrow moustaches – report to your wig centre without delay.

Hair weaving, in which strands of existing hair are knitted into a mat over the bald patch, is highly thought of by some. In the same way, hair transplants, whereby follicle-bearing plugs are planted like little tomatoes across the naked area, have achieved wide recognition – provided one is careful to tell the operative to transplant only from elsewhere on the head. There are certain cut-price clinics in Tangier and Tijuana which take it from what I can only describe as other sites. The results, while undeniably hairy, are disconcerting.

If you are in straits, there is always the low parting, in which the hair of one side of the head is allowed to grow twelve inches or so and then pasted over the bald patch with brilliantine. The moment to cease this

manoeuvre is when you discover that your parting has to make an upward detour or meander to avoid your ear. The low parting is unstable in high winds, and hard to repair *sur le champ*.

Final recourse is to shave the head. Remember this: a receding hairline adds distinction, but *nobody has ever seen or should ever see a partially bald bounder*.

COSMETICS

There exist a number of quite unreasonable prejudices against the wearing of cosmetics by men. Ridiculously, this even extends to the use of the many deliciously scented toilet preparations currently available. Just as there is no harm in providing nose-joy for all you meet, there is no reason not to cover up blemishes with a light coating of some suitable enamel or blusher. These grooming aids are particularly helpful if you have a really offensive feature such as a scar or a nose rendered scarlet and bulbous by overindulgence in the good things of life. A little practice will enable you to avoid the undesirable raddled look (often achieved by beginners) and regain your youthful bloom.

FINISHING TOUCHES

Once you are correctly dressed, shod, jewelled, coiffed and groomed, you will be ready to face the world. Or will you? However dapper the outer man, the inner man must be kept confident. Two indispensable aids to confidence, often forgotten, are good teeth and hands. An excellent denture fixative can be obtained for a few coppers; hands should be serviced regularly by a good manicurist (but make sure you use only clear – never coloured – nail polish). If you bite your nails, wear gloves.

Of course, little sartorial accidents will happen. I myself was unfortunate enough (or that was how I saw it at the time) to lose my false teeth during a discussion with my secretary in the back seat of Vauxhall Victor I once sold in Catford. Not without trepidation, I travelled to the Cheam address of the undergardener to whom I sold the car. The trepidation was justified.

I approached the car unobserved, and regained the denture. As I reinstated it, however, the odd-job man emerged from the stables, where I gather he had been trying to make telephonic contact with me to complain about the quantity of oil-soaked oatmeal he had discovered in the gearbox after its failure. I was forced in the ensuing chase to shin up the wisteria on the large house adjoining, where I found myself in the boudoir of the daughter of the undergardener's employer. Her name was Enid Catchpole; soon afterwards I resigned from Catford Used Vauxhalls. The rest is history.

AUTOMOBILISM

The matter of cars is so straightforward that very little needs to be said. Centrally, a car expresses the real you. You are therefore selling yourself short if you own anything that is not a Jaguar with an engine capacity of three litres or above. One realizes that Rollers have their apologists, and that your Euro-bounder feels a lack of fulfilment when not at the wheel of a Merc. My view – and I admit that it is the view of a traditionalist – is that Rollers reek of villainy and that Mercs are for Germans and ladies, God bless them. Jags have it all: Sebring Red is nice and cheery, the seats lend themselves to a bit of ocelot or leopard, and there is masses of power under that bonnet for a quick getaway with your trousers round your ankles and the Dobermans at your heels. Also, long habit has made me adept at rapid concupiscence in the Jag, whereas the times I have tried it in anything else have been difficult and dangerous – as, for instance, in the case of the Vauxhall Victor and the false teeth.

Now that all cars look alike, it is a temptation to shrug the shoulders and maintain that since they are all the same, it doesn't matter a damn which one you drive. Wrong, terribly wrong. For instance, to the knowledgeable, a *Ford* implies that if you are not a roller towel rep you have certainly been one at some point in your life; a *Japanese* car of any make, that you are a deaf midget; a *Citroën* or a *Renault*, that you are about to chain yourself to the reactor at your nearest nuclear power station; a *Rover*, that you are a company director in a company that actually makes something; a *Volvo*, that you are a bent antique dealer.

But in a Jag, you're a bounder.

I rest my case.

7
Talking Your Way to the Top

It is no good expending time and effort on your personal appearance if at the end of it you are going to hide your glory behind a newspaper in a bus queue in Hendon. Once you are satisfied with the way you look, it is time to attack the citadels of society. The only way of doing this is by talking to people, preferably in places where drink is available. Public houses provide a reasonable starting ground for the tyro, but after a while it will become apparent that few of real power and influence frequent such places. Private parties are the only solution.

But how, I hear someone say, will I get asked to such parties?

An extraordinarily foolish question. You will not get asked. You will simply go.

But is this not gate-crashing?

Of course it is. There is nothing wrong with gate-crashing, except that you may find yourself being hurled into Belgrave Square by bouncers at 11 p.m. The best way to get round this is to start with *cocktail parties*, which are very seldom guarded by bouncers. They can be found fairly easily. Simply roam the streets of the better parts of London, ears peeled for the roar of conversation and eyes alert for the parabolae of unwanted *canapés* from upper windows. Insinuate yourself, smiling broadly, and start talking. If anyone asks who you are, claim that Arthur brought you. If their name turns out to be Arthur, point out another one. Maintain jauntiness until someone asks you to *their* cocktail party, next Tuesday. You should find that the thing snowballs rapidly after that; experts spend an average of one evening per year at home, if indeed they have a home at all. The only essentials are an excellent appearance, a flashing smile and remorseless flow of small talk.

SMALL TALK: THE GROUND RULES

The most difficult part of small talk is beginning. Subjects like the weather, recent plays and important books are rapidly exhausted. The ensuing silence is

normally filled with gossip, but if the gathering into which you have insinuated yourself consists of complete strangers, you are hardly going to have your finger on the pulse. Two techniques suggest themselves here. The first and best is to listen closely for the *dominant voice*. This will probably be female. A truly dominant voice rises above the general roar and does not pause for breath. Its conversational partners wear a glazed expression and will be only too happy to edge away as you approach. Once you set it going by asking it, for example, who is that man with the terrible squint, it will fill you in on the hopes, fears, aspirations and infidelities of everyone in the room before it gets round to trying to find out who you are, by which time you will in turn have edged away.

The second technique is the *Royal Insight*, in which a perfect stranger is bombarded with your observations on the inner workings of the Household. This works well with older women, who will form an exaggerated opinion of your connections and insist on introducing you to their daughters, who will probably be of an age to ask you to dinner parties.

Naturally one likes to get drunk at cocktail parties.

A word of warning: drunk is fine, but beastly drunk is not. It is difficult to appear in a good light when you are lying unconscious in a bath under a dozen Bollinger and a foot of crushed ice.

As you find your feet in society, conversation becomes more demanding. While the actual content of your remarks is not significant, correct language is. The conventions of your chosen group can be picked up rapidly – usages such as loo for toilet, sofa for settee, drawing room for lounge, should be carefully noted, as solecisms may actually be more damaging to your prospects than a fit of vomiting on the Aubusson. If in doubt, masquerade as a colonial of some kind. Colonials may be frightfully charlie and unaware of correct conduct at a cockers pee, as they are, well, such a *breath of fresh air*. Students requiring a closer knowledge of cocktail-party language are recommended to read the books of Evelyn Waugh and Nancy Mitford, as well as *Harpers and Queen*.

Cocktail parties lie at the foundations of social activity. There are other approaches which serve to impress listeners with the fact that you are a superior individual.

Talking Your Way to the Top

1 *Talking dirty*   At its simplest, this takes the form of sprinkling your conversation with four-letter words, thereby suggesting that though well bred and educated you are still in touch with the masses and probably a born leader of men. More advanced dirty talkers eschew four-letter words, however, preferring to attract attention with a fund of diverting yarns based on the excretory and reproductive processes and a crisp insight into the characteristics of the various races, particularly those from southern and eastern nations. As I implied earlier, the cultivation of merriness during your school career lays a firm foundation for such talk.

2 *Creative boringness*   A valuable technique for those who find it difficult to remember smutty stories, this depends for this effectiveness on the fact that all the world loves an expert. The bore holds forth at length on the subject of his choice, which should be unfamiliar to his listeners. Knowledge of this subject is not important; what is vital is the acquisition of a store of *buzz* words. These are words invented by cliques to make simple ideas sound large, mysterious and daunting, or alternatively to make an unproven hypothesis sound

like a *fait accompli*, or alternatively, to mean nothing at all. Personally I am inclined to subscribe to the latter type and have had great success with the Chance Charts, which I now make available to you in truncated form.

HOW TO USE THE CHANCE CHARTS
Select a word from each column. String them together, puff out the chest and force them across the teeth with an air of deep conviction. Best used after the port.

Chance Charts: Buzz words

Military – industrial – agricultural
(no. of possible combinations: 512)

hard	sin	surplus
soft	conversion	deficit
bloody	Russian	interface
liveweight	currency	situation
deadweight	response	index
pig	weapon	headache
North–South	trade	dialogue
overkill	destabilization	tendency

Talking Your Way to the Top

Arts (no. of possible combinations: 512)

beautiful	tension	disease
solid	whimsy	workshop
lapidary	reportage	theatre
terse	brushwork	inherency
incoherent	Weltschmertz	feats
seal-like	tennis shoe	relationship
gay	pride	obesity
foot	succumbed	quality

In my own view it is by no means the least feat of Hockney to achieve this relationship between whimsy and Weltschmertz.

New technology (no. of possible combinations: 729)

program	download	interface
software	net	facility
hardware	disk	capability
menu	search	data
RAM	accessing	drive
direct	input	enhancement
sodding	sales	man
mother	in	law
mainframe	terminal	key

Sporting landowners (no. of possible combinations: 6)

bloody	Blair
bloody	EU
bloody	Americans
bloody	Hell
bloody	good port old boy
bloody	er, forgotten what I was goin' to say

PRONUNCIATION – A BRIEF NOTE

More has been written about correct pronunciation than about any other aspect of bounding. The original test, probably devised by Alexander Pope, consists of the repetition of the phrase: 'Thousands and thousands of Boy Scouts bounding around in brown trousers.' Meaningless, you may say; yet these syllables convey more about the speaker than several volumes of autobiography.

Those whose modes of speech were formed between the years 1945-68 should pronounce in the Churchillian manner, thus: 'Thowsands and thowsands of Bory Scowts bownding arownd in browwn trowsers,' forming the 'ow' sound by making a tight circle with the lips and keeping the tongue stiff, but not tremulous.

Younger pronouncers may prefer the equally prestigious but somehow brisker: 'Thighsands and thighsands of Buy Skites binding arinde in brine tryzers.' These sounds are accomplished with a baring of the clenched teeth, stretched but immobile lips, and a discreet wagging of the tongue behind the ivory fence. It is a technique that has recently gained popularity with Conservative back benchers, as it is always extremely difficult to tell who is talking. And, of course, for such MPs, the natural expression of the face in repose is the rictus described above.

The natural tendency of most of us is to say
'Theaousands and theaousands of Boigh Skeaouts
beaounding areaound in breaouwn trousers.' While
this is to be discouraged, discreet interjection of such
sounds into the discourse can disorient and threaten
the hearer. Salesmen seem to find it a particularly
useful gambit. In my view this fear is produced by an
atavistic race memory of the premiership of Edward
Heath, a disorienting period in human history if ever
there was one.

There are few circumstances in which regional or
working-class pronunciations are permissible, though
it is admittedly useful to have a reasonable stock of
them in the repertoire. They are most useful on the
telephone when financial restraint has made it
necessary to dispense with the butler or other
intermediary. Milos Stugeron, of whom I have spoken
before, carried mimicry into the realms of high art,
being able in times of stress to imitate two crossed lines
and a fault in the exchange, which made it possible for
him to terminate even the most delicate calls in mid-
sentence, attempts to reconnect being met with his
virtuoso imitation of the 'number unobtainable' signal.

BIG TALK

A sound grasp of the principles of small talk should leave you with an air of authority as visible as the fogs that cling to the shoulders of Mount Fuji, as well as a reputation for charm and good nature. A talent for small talk is no use in isolation, however; there will come a dread hour when reckonings have to be paid, and deals closed. At this point you will have to make the transition into *talking big*.

Much big talk is a matter for individual initiative. If, for instance, you are trying to convince shareholders that next year's performance will be an improvement on this year's £40 million operating loss, there is no sense in a pawky forecast of reduced losses. Let it be known that you confidently expect £100 million profit, to which end all directors' fees are being waived and you are actively considering takeover bids for Shell Petroleum, Barclays Bank and Equitable Life. This will put a spring in the step of the assembled shareholders; any personal sacrifices in the way of directors' fees can be made up by creative accounting procedures.

NAME DROPPING

Probably the most efficient form of big talk is *name dropping*, a practice that has origins in far antiquity, when individuals invoked various deities in the hope that mention of self and deity in the same sentence would confer upon self attributes of the deity. This seldom worked, but it instilled confidence in the invoker and any who happened to be listening.

Choosing a name

If you are trying to sell a car, the prospective buyer may

I WAS HAVING A LITTLE NECTAR WITH HERMES WHEN WHO SHOULD DROP BY BUT ZEUS.

be led to think more highly of the vehicle if you mention to him that Niki Lauda dropped in last week and said he wished he had one of those.

When selecting a name to drop, ask yourself the following questions:

1 Will the target recognize the name?
2 Does the target know the droppee socially, and if so will he or she check up?
3 Is the droppee category-specific?

If the answer to questions 1 and 3 is 'yes' and question 2 'no', go ahead, and good luck to you.

There are three main techniques of name dropping, each excellent. They may be used singly or permed. The golden rule is to start simply, adding refinements and twists as your confidence increases. Those who find that they rely to a large extent on this technique may find it beneficial to keep a notebook in which one page is allotted per target. List names already dropped, and also names that for one reason or another should not be used.

1 *The simple drop with optional curriculum vitae*   At its most basic this is the 'As I was saying to Heseltine the other day, what the world needs at this point is a digital pop-up toaster.' This not only implies that you are on easy terms with Michael Heseltine, but also that he is in the habit of asking your advice on matters of importance. It also flatters your listener by giving him the impression that were you, he and Michael Heseltine in the same room together, you would certainly between you thrash out something pretty significant about the problems of the British electrical goods industry.

The optional curriculum vitae is used when your target may be unfamiliar with the droppee, or when you wish to give the target the impression that you have no great opinion of his intelligence; thus: 'As I was saying to Michael Heseltine the other day, you may remember the chap, used to be in the Tory cabinet, buys furniture, things are in a bit of a mess.'

NOTE: *Who's Who* is the name dropper's bible. Of course, I know almost everybody in the volume intimately, but even I admit that in early life I spent half an hour a day boning up a page, by rote. Never be without it.

2 *Story appropriation*   A superficially simple gambit, but one requiring a fair degree of inventiveness. The dropper selects a well-known incident in the life of a famous name, and claims to have been present, narrating the anecdote from his own point of view. Thus: 'Yes, how well one recalls Tiger Marks. I remember the night they took him away, blood everywhere of course, but then – well, I'd better not tell you his name but suffice it to say he had concrete in his turnups when he came back. Yes, whenever I drive across the Hammersmith Flyover I shed a little tear for poor old Tig, as we used to call him. Had a wonderful baritone, did you know that?'

3 *The prime mover drop*   In this well-loved technique, the dropper claims responsibility for starting a chain of events that rocked the world. Thus: 'Do you know a while back I was talking to Ronnie Reagan and he happened to say that he had never seen Mount Rushmore? Well, of course, I flew him right over and he was most impressed, and after that I caught him sneaking glimpses of his profile in the vanity mirror in the Cadillac and I thought, well, hell, you know actors.

But then he turned to me and he said: "Harry," he said, "there's a big old lump of rock up yonder and it kind of reminds me of me.' And I guess that was the start of it all.'

With time and application, a really good name dropper can acquire the reputation of being a man who knows everybody, advise the great, and has a tremendous fund of original ideas. There is a mystery to name dropping similar to that of Count Cagliostro, who always seemed to slip into the group photograph at the last moment, slipping away immediately afterwards. The cries of 'Who he?' swiftly changed to 'Ah, Cagliostro. Sound fellow.'

Sound fellows can get away with *anything*.

RUMOUR-MONGERING
Name dropping is a splendid way of building yourself up. There are times, however, when it is necessary to scupper those who do not see things your way. The quickest way is violence; but for those with an instinctive shrinking from this a rumour is only slightly slower-

acting and will probably be more effective in the long run. There are two main methods of mongering a rumour to the detriment of an opponent. The first is the saturation rumour, by which a slander is so widely repeated that the target is forced to throw up his job, grow a beard, change his name, acquire a false passport and leave the country. The second is the precision or pinpoint rumour, being a slander which may be of interest to only one other person besides the target, but which has a devastating effect.

1 *Saturation rumour-mongering* Most journalism is now saturation rumour-mongering, and the technique has achieved the status of an art form. Once you have invented your rumour, send anonymous letters to the press. This body will stick its foot in the target's door and commence speculating. Since the state education system has rendered a vast sector of the public incapable of rational thought, such speculations are soon accepted as gospel truth.

A fine example of saturation rumour-mongering is the spy fever that occasionally grips the populace. A putative ninth, tenth, or eleventh man can be publicly pilloried on the strength of a memo suggesting that he was once seen drinking vodka with a picture restorer who was known to have a conviction for soliciting in a gents in Peckham.

The old adage suggests that if you throw enough mud, some of it will stick. This method ensures that the mud arrives in a JCB bucket and does not so much stick as flatten.

2 *Precision rumour-mongering*   This has long been a favourite technique with female bounders. Classically, the rumour is started by a bitch and an accomplice, speaking in the hearing of (but not *to*) the target's spouse. The bitch makes an allegation concerning the blond hairs the dry cleaner noticed on target's coat collar, or the supposed resemblance of target's last child to the milkman. The mongerer will have been speaking in high, indignant tones, cutting herself off short on 'becoming aware' of target spouse's presence. Target and spouse can then be confidently expected to be living in separate accommodation within the month.

Envoi

The wind is still rustling the palmettoes. In one hand a glass of rum jingles musically. With the other I make ready to lay down my pen; this long road we have travelled together winds to its close. For me, life will continue – the challenge of the nightly bezique game, the soft cooing of an absent friend's wife well consoled, the dividend briefcases of crisp fivers arriving on the noon plane. For you, gentle reader, the future is less predictable. All I can say is that I have given you the tools, and it is up to you to finish the job.

The sun is sinking over the Caribbean now. Far to the east, Catford sleeps, the City of London diverts itself in casinos with Arabs, and Wentworth swaps wives. Over there comes a dreaminess, a nostalgia that causes tears to prick gently behind the dark glasses; a sense that having started as a missionary, one has finished almost as a father.

It puts me in mind of something my own father said

to me long ago, after he had told me about the birds and the bees.

'If you believe the foregoing, cocky,' he said, 'you will believe bleeding anything.'

Quite so.

Farewell.

Harry Chance
Villa Borghese
Grand Cayman
2000

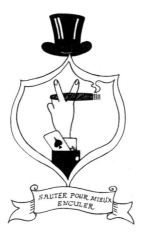

SAUTER POUR MIEUX ENCULER

APPENDIX ONE
Five Acceptable Public Schools

ETON

Ties: numerous. Best to stick to Old Etonian, black with diagonal light blue stripes.

Advantages: Eton contains about twelve hundred pupils, so if you are assuming Old Etonianhood you stand only a small chance of getting rumbled. Signs of Old Etonians are poise and self-confidence, advantageous for used car-salesmen and those whose personal habits lead them to fall over at social gatherings. Since the school is located a short walk from an excellent railway station, London is within easy reach.

WINCHESTER

Ties: Black, navy-blue and brown wide strips.

Advantages: Winchester is a sort of laboratory in

which little boys are altered until they are civil service mandarins. The rest of the world is therefore terrified of the place. If you have a high forehead and an uncontrollable nervous tic, and are finding it hard to make your way in the world as a result of these disabilities, Winchester is the school for you. People who have been at Winchester are called Wykehamists. One day they will be pure brain, ghastly great eggs covered in a sort of Virginia creeper of pulsing blue veins.

GORDONSTOUN

Ties: narrow white, mauve and white stripes on a pale blue background (or open collar, displaying huge bronzed throat).

Advantages: this school possesses its own fire brigade, and is located in a howling Scottish wilderness from which the only egress is by rowing boat. It therefore produces vast human beings with booming laughs, much given to issuing vice-like handshakes with paws calloused to a depth of three inches. Gordonstouners very seldom fall down themselves, but rove restlessly on the fringes of parties looking for people who have, so they can rescue them.

HARROW

Tie: Old Harrovian is dark blue with pairs of narrow oblique white stripes.

Advantages: very few people seem to know anything at all about Harrow, except that its inmates wear boaters. It is close to London but there is no example recorded of a Harrovian actually visiting the City. The best that can be said of it is that it has a conveniently solid anonymity, and that there is a school farm. A bit of chat about the school farm might get you out of a tight corner at the Oddfellow's Hall, Suckley-cum-Postgate, if you are fool enough to go there in the first place.

MILLFIELD

Tie: not known. This is an excellent school but one at which ties are regarded as having little meaning.

Advantages: opinions differ as to whether this really

is a school. I have included it because it caters for geniuses and morons alike; for instance, if you excel at steeplechasing you will be given to a steeplechasing tutor and be winning Olympic medals before you can say 'final straight'. It is not clear whether or not they accept bounding as a developable skill, though one or two Old Millfieldians of my acquaintance lead me to believe that there must be an excellent bounding tutor on the staff. Its diversity makes it a useful alma mater of convenience for those of us who are incurable rough diamonds.

APPENDIX TWO
Acceptable Regiments

A lot of unnecessary fuss is made about regiments. Some people claim to have been members of the Black Watch, the Rifle Brigade, and similarly exotic trained bands. This leads only to confusion.

Really acceptable regiments are to be found only in the Brigade of Guards. No matter if you are a midget; only other ranks need to fulfil the height criterion. All you require are the courage of a lion and family connections with the adjutant of one of the regiments (or failing this, a glib tongue and a Guards tie).

The Guards tie is red and blue stripes. The knot is tied to present the blue above the red – do not ask me why. Get it anywhere in Jermyn Street.

REGIMENTAL NICKNAMES

Scots Guards: Jocks
Irish Guards: Micks

Appendix Two

Coldstream Guards: Sheepshaggers
Grenadier Guards: Gobblers (presumably through some past connection with turkeys, or there again not)
Blues and Royal (Horse Guards): None (can usually ride)
Life Guards: Galloping Grocers, Grocers (can usually ride)

APPENDIX THREE
How Do You Bound?

Answer the following questions to the best of your ability. Time allowed: 5 minutes.

1 When did you last help a little old lady cross the road?

(a) yesterday or more recently
(b) when in the Scouts
(c) mind your own business

2 You are in Hong Kong, lunching with a rich property developer and a beautiful RSPCA inspector. Dog is on the menu. Do you

(a) walk out of the restaurant?
(b) order the dish and, when it arrives, pat and caress it?
(c) order a bottle of whisky to get you over the shock, make your companions drunk, persuade the developer

to open a vegetarian restaurant in which you will have shares, and spend the afternoon in fornication with the RSPCA inspector?

3 A small child approaches you, begging alms. Do you

(a) slip it a fiver?
(b) kick it in the mazzard?
(c) come to an arrangement with it that it will distribute dodgy £20 notes for you on commission?

4 An elderly relation, alcoholic and suffering from heart trouble, has made a will in your favour. Do you

(a) visit the bedside and attempt to lighten his final hours with holy discourse?
(b) send him two dozen old brandy and a drum of benzedrine, and keep your fingers crossed?
(c) sell your interest in the estate to a man you meet in a public house?

5 A perfect stranger accosts you while he is drowning in a canal. Your instant reaction is to

(a) dive in, offering immediate aid and succour?

(b) rush for a lifebelt, inform the police, ambulance and clergy, and then lend carefully considered assistance?
(c) continue down the towpath, averting the eyes, since you have not been introduced?

6 Orange socks are worn with dinner jackets. Is this

(a) true?
(b) false?
(c) a lovely idea?

7 The basic function of the human shoe is to

(a) exclude cold and moisture from the human foot?
(b) resemble a double portion of exotic ice cream?
(c) hint at its owner's sexual and intellectual prowess?

8 On hearing the phrase 'eternal triangle', do you immediately think of

(a) lawyer, lawyer, co-respondent?
(b) man, woman, man?
(c) man, woman, woman?
(d) the percussion part of L. Welk's arrangement of 'Raindrops Keep Falling on My Head'?

9 Most of your friends have been married for

(a) less than a year?
(b) more than two years?
(c) so long that all they know is they have been down so long it looks like up to them?

10 The most desirable attribute of a spouse-to-be is

(a) perfect physique?
(b) a small bottom?
(c) five-star fornicatory attributes?
(d) none of these?

11 Your perambulator is left unattended in Kensington Gardens while your nanny chatters with Nanny de Vere Pendergast. Do you

(a) exchange prams and clothes with Clarence de VP (six months)?
(b) exchange clothes only, returning to your own pram?
(c) scream like a banshee because nobody is paying any attention to you?

12 It is midnight. You are on the roof of your preparatory school enjoying a rapid gasper. The headmaster apprehends you, asking for an explanation. You replay

(a) smiling winningly, that your restlessly inquiring nature has long been needling you to experiment with nicotine?

(b) that he has ten seconds to say his prayers because after that he will be over the parapet with a slug in his belly?

(c) that you heard the plaintive mewing of Matron's cat, which loves the smell of cigarette smoke, and came aloft to rescue same. You then produce Mato's cat, kidnapped for just such an eventuality, from under your dressing gown?

13 The GCSE candidate's armoury is best stocked with

(a) facts?

(b) postage-stamp-sized editions of well-known textbooks?

(c) disappearing ink?

14 You are offered 7000 preference shares in a South African mining concern at 4.5p. with takeover prospects and a subsequent one-for-one option. Do you

(a) sell them long?
(b) sell them short?
(c) buy a dictionary?
(d) in view of the uncertainty of all things, remove the decimal point from the quotation with a rubber and sell the lot to a dear friend?

15 Your bank manager sends you a letter requesting an urgent interview about the state of your overdraft. Do you

(a) send him a large present of ivory, apes and peacocks?
(b) refuse point blank, on the grounds that you find it hard to get on with menials of any kind?
(c) agree and proceed to interview with your briefcase bulging with life-insurance policies and negotiable securities?

16 You have borrowed a fiver off a man who subsequently saves you from drowning. On the banks of the river you notice that his underwear is ragged and his limbs shrunken with poverty. Do you

(a) pay him the fiver?
(b) jump back into the river?
(c) Refuse to pay him the fiver on the grounds that friendship and finance do not mix?

17 The aeroplane in which you are a passenger is sixty seconds away from impact with the southern slopes of Mount Kenya. You grab

(a) a nun?
(b) a stewardess's thigh?
(c) a roll of lavatory paper?

18 You are hiding in a wardrobe as a cuckolded husband cocks his Uzi in the bedroom beyond. In the wardrobe are hanging four uniforms, all your size. You choose

(a) the Scots Guards?

(b) the Sisters of Mercy?
(c) the trappists?
(d) Superman?

19 You are evicted from your house, you write off the Jag, your bird is up the spout, and several rubber cheques are demonstrating the homing instinct. Do you

(a) change your name?
(b) join the staff of a certain used-car firm in South London?
(c) leave the country?

20 You are offered £500 if you will

(a) smuggle 50 kilos of cocaine into Iran (where the death penalty obtains for such activities) by a known informer
(b) substitute for the world snake-sitting champion who has pulled out of his current challenge due to fatal blood poisoning

Which would you choose?

SOLUTION

Regrettably, there is no easy way of confronting the harsh realities of life; they cannot, for instance, be properly encapsulated in quiz form, whatever women's magazines and tabloid newspapers would have you believe. But some of you may be disappointed if, having burned brain cells and pencil lead, you are not patted on the back.

So well done all of you for having got this far. Reward yourselves with a stiff bracer of some kind.

Now for the bad news.

If you have answered any of the questions at all, you have failed. Only a rank idiot would commit himself to a response to a purely hypothetical state of affairs. *Sur le champ* is the only place to be.

Score 5 points for each question answered. Scores of more than 40 qualify you for an opportunity to purchase accommodation in Mosquito Coast Nirvana Condominiums. Just send me your name, address and money. I'll see to the rest!